# COLONIAL STATE, CAPITAL AND LABOUR IN INDIA

In Memory of Prof. Bipan Chandra

# COLONIAL STATE, CAPITAL AND LABOUR IN INDIA

*Edited by*

**K. Venugopal Reddy**

KALPAZ

ISBN : 978-93-5128-035-4

Price : ₹ 670

First Published, 2015

*Published by*

Kalpaz Publications
C-30, Satyawati Nagar,
Delhi-110052
Ph. : 9212142040
E-mail: kalpaz@hotmail.com

*Laser Typesetting* : Gyan Print (AB-II), Delhi
*Printed at* : G. Print Process, Delhi

**Cataloging in Publication Data—DK**
Courtesy: D.K. Agencies (P) Ltd. <docinfo@dkagencies.com>

**National Seminar on 'Colonial State, Capital and Labour in India' (2011 : Department of History, Pondicherry University)**
Colonial state, capital and labour in India / edited by K. Venugopal Reddy.
p. cm.
Includes bibliographical references and index.
ISBN 9789351280354

1. Labor—India—History—Congresses. 2. Working class—India—History—Congresses. 3. Capitalism—India—History—Congresses. 4. India—Politics and government—19th century—Congresses. I. Venugopal Reddy, K. (Kanchi), 1962- II. Title.

DDC 331.0954 23

# Contents

# Preface

The foundation of British colonial rule in the mid-eighteenth century remains a defining moment in the history of India. It heralded significant changes in diverse fields of Indian society and economy. The colonial state which was established in India functioned primarily for the advantage of the British colonisers. The book makes a modest endeavour to unravel some of the transformations that the colonial state brought in and their impact. The book is based on the papers presented at the national seminar on 'Colonial State, Capital and Labour in India' organised in March 2011 at the Department of History, Pondicherry University. My special thanks are to the Indian Council of Historical Research, New Delhi and Pondicherry University, Puducherry for their financial and all other kinds of necessary support extended in organising the event. I am highly indebted to Prof. Chandra Krishnamurthy, Vice Chancellor, Pondicherry University, Puducherry for her encouragement in bringing out the book. Also I am equally indebted to Prof. J.A.K. Tareen, for having inspired me to organise the national seminar, which only made the publication of the book possible.

I am indeed grateful to Prof. Bipan Chandra, who also remains a fountain of my academic and intellectual activities. Further I convey my deep sense of indebtedness to Prof. Sabyasachi Bhattacharya, former Chairman, ICHR, New Delhi, Prof. Aditya Mukherjee and Prof. Mridula Mukherjee for their constant encouragement and support in bringing out the book.

I express my deep sense of gratitude to my colleagues at the Department of History, Pondicherry University for their unstinted cooperation and support in all of my intellectual forays. Prof. G. Chandhrika, Head, Dept. of History, Pondicherry University remains as ever a great source of encouragement and motivation in getting the work published. I particularly thank her for it. I also thank Prof. Venkata Raghotham, Prof. K. Rajan and other faculty colleagues at the Department for their sustained support during the course of the publication of the book. I remain very much beholden to my other faculty colleagues at the School of Social Sciences and International Studies, Pondicherry University for their constant encouragement for all of my intellectual activities. Particularly I extend my thanks to Prof. N.K. Jha, Dean, School of Social Sciences and International Studies, Prof. B.B. Mohanty, Head, Dept. of Sociology, Prof. B. Mohanan Pillai, Dept. of Politics, Prof. B. Krishna Murthy, Chairman, Centre for European Studies, Prof. Murthy, Head, Dept. of Politics.

Above all, I am extremely grateful to the contributors for having responded to my call to revise their papers and send them to me in time. Their eagerness to revise the papers and patient responses have greatly facilitated the timely publication of the book. I extend my special thanks to the students and other supporting staff of the Dept. of History, Pondicherry University for all the help extended during the publication of the work.

I am highly grateful to the Kalpaz Publications, Delhi, for accepting my proposal immediately and seeing the publication of the book well in time.

**K. Venugopal Reddy**

# List of Contributors

**K. Venugopal Reddy,** Department of History, Pondicherry University, India.

**G. Chandhrika,** Department of History, Pondicherry University, Puducherry, India.

**Devireddy Subramanyam Reddy (Retd.),** Department of History, S.V. University, Tirupati, Andhra Pradesh, India.

**Shri Krishan,** Department of History, Post-Graduate Regional Centre (M.D. University), Rewari, Haryana, India.

**Movva Srinivasa Reddy,** Department of History, Andhra Loyola College, (Autonomous) Vijayawada, Andhra Pradesh, India.

**Manoj Kumar Sahoo,** Doctoral Scholar, Center for Historical Studies, Jawaharlal Nehru University, New Delhi, India.

**A. Suresh,** Department of History, Pondicherry University, Puducherry, India.

**Bibin Kuriakose,** Doctoral Scholar, Center for Historical Studies, Jawaharlal Nehru University, New Delhi, India.

*K. Venugopal Reddy*

# 1

# Colonial State, Capital and Labour in India

## Introduction

The phenomenon of Colonialism, though not uniform in the colonised spaces globally, unleashed the consequences, which were ubiquitously disastrous for the people. It has destroyed possibilities of social, economic, political and cultural advancement in the colonised space. Hence 'the development of underdevelopment' has been the trajectory of Colonialism in African, Latin American or Asian countries, though it might vary from one site to the other.[1]

The process of the establishment of colonial state in India was simultaneously followed by the process of delegitimation of pre-colonial authority in political life and "the obverse of the process, the appropriation of the insignia of authority by the colonial state from the pre-existing indigenous inventory. The delegitimation process was instantiated in innumerable displacement of individuals and institutions empowered by pre-colonial history."[2] The formation of colonial state in India was laid in the crucible of ruthless violence. The colonial state, once consolidated its position through 'conquest, rule and administration,'[3] had embarked on to refashion Indian society, which became the 'experimental site'.[4] And therefore the colonial state justified the introduction of 'new institutions, regulations or practices'[5] with particular emphasis on India's political, economic and social backwardness in the past.

The process of ordering what was considered 'disorderly'[6] was a protracted and painful process as the colonial state endeavoured to alter or disorganise the Indian economy, in the process, distort the society and disorient the patterns of development. Thus colonialism had only played a destructive role in India's social, political and economic evolution and contributed, in particular, to 'the development of underdevelopment'. This process has only engendered widespread resistance from all sections of Indian society, particularly the subalterns. The colonial state, functioned with sole objective of systematic exploitation of immense resources devising varied instruments to subordinate Indian economy, and society. The book focuses on the interrogation of the foundation and the function of colonial state in India's social, political and economic evolution. The tardy and stunted nature of India's industrial growth bears ample evidence for colonial state's negligence to develop the native industry in India. The book, while focusing on the formation of colonial state and its role in 'the development of underdevelopment' in India, aims to explore the emergence of new social classes and the dynamics of development.

The book explores the anti-colonial responses of labour in diverse contexts and varied spaces. It seeks to explore the issues of enduring relevance to the understanding of nature of colonial state and of technologies employed by the colonial state to co-opt or subjugate the labour in India. It focuses on the process of spontaneous and organised expressions of discontent against colonial oppression, domination and marginalisation and how they turned into institutionalised movement. It also endeavours to articulate on the rise of industrial labour, the development of trade unions and their solidarity to anti-colonial struggle. The book on 'Colonial State, Capital and Labour in India' therefore seeks to interrogate this excruciating process, unmasking the technologies employed by the British colonial state to enfeeble or emasculate India. The papers which are presented here explore the multiple dimensions of the theme 'Colonial State, Capital and Labour in India'.

K. Venugopal Reddy in his paper on 'Colonial State in India: A Critical Appraisal' interrogates the nature of colonial state and the resistance engendered from subaltern sections, particularly the peasants, industrial workers and the tribals. He delineates sharply how colonised Indians were perceived and projected as 'barbaric' or 'uncivilised' by the British colonisers and how the characterisation of India in deprecatory mould was used to justify their existence in India. India was constructed and projected as a land bereft of any progressive quality.

The paper examines the architecture of dominance of colonial state. Resistance of the colonised was engendered by the coloniser. The native resistance followed colonial dominance as both the processes were interconnected and interlinked. The paper explores the multiple sites of resistance and demonstrates how they owe to the colonial state. Focus is laid on delineating the nature of contradiction between the colonised Indians and the British colonisers. The nature of this basic contradiction underlying British colonial rule in India constituted the core of the relationship between Indians, particularly the subaltern classes, and the British. The revolt of 1857 symbolised this growing disillusionment of Indians with the existence and continuation of British colonial rule in India.

Colonialism necessarily produces the conditions of resistance. The exploitative economic policies, the suppressive anti-labour measures, and the rapacious and interventionist agenda of colonial state vis-à-vis peasants, industrial workers and tribal communities, respectively, had constituted the critical components in the saga of the resistance movement throughout colonial India. The paper endeavours to present this trajectory of resistance of peasants, industrial working class and the tribal communities against colonial state in India.

G. Chandhrika in her paper on 'Capitalism, Colonial State and Indentured Labour from India' critically looks at the roots of Indentured Labour system in India and demonstrates how British colonial rule facilitated migration of labour to British West Indies. British Imperialism in the age of global capitalism provided the ideological, political and legal justification for economic exploitation of colonies. In India, the British colonial state claimed to have brought civilisation and modernity to colonised people. This paper argues indentured system of labour, regulated by British Indian colonial state, constituted a labour subject under legally encoded conditions as free labour, but in actuality translated as unfree labour. Not much different from slavery, this form of labour legitimized the use of coercive power in tapping labour resources from India for promotion of British economic interests. She argues Indentured Labour from India replaced slave labour in sugar plantations of British West Indies, India thus, became the main source of labour supply to planter colonies of the European colonial empires, she concludes.

Devireddy Subramanyam Reddy in his paper on 'Emergence of Landless Class in Colonial Southern India' demonstrates how new classes of people came into existence during the British colonial rule, which include the landed classes like Zamindari proprietors (not owners) of land (both aristocratic as well as moneyocratic Zamindars), Pattadari proprietors (not owners) of land, non-agriculturist landlords from various professions, tenants (paying rent in money or kind), sharecroppers (sharers in crop with proprietors of land), agricultural labourers (free or hired or seasonal labourers), bonded labourers, serfs and the merchant bourgeois or middle class, industrial capitalists, finance capitalists, industrial working class, as well as the intelligentsia. He maintains that as modern Indian society is vast, the present paper confines to the aspects of creation or emergence of landless class during British colonial period. It attempts more particularly with the role of Ryotwari land revenue system in southern India in contributing to the emergence of landless class like tenants, share croppers, agricultural labourers, bonded labourers, serfs, etc.

Shri Krishan in his paper on 'World of Labour and Capital: Analysis of Gandhi's Political-Ideological Forms' explores several ways of looking at the relation between Gandhi and indigenous capitalist class as well as labour. He argues initially that Gandhi was regarded as a 'bourgeois agent' who clothed his ideology in peasant populist clothes. He is seen as the leader of a political formation which led multi-class anti-imperialist democratic revolution. Some point out high degree of ambiguity in Gandhi's relation to different social classes. He argues that Gandhi's synthesis of peasant millenarianism and 'bourgeois-rationality' has been evaluated differently. The Subaltern Studies collective highlighted the tensions and contestation between nationalism and 'subaltern' social groups and communities.

However, still there is some scope for investigation of complexities of political-ideological forms evolved under the leadership of Gandhi, and ambiguities they represent. Gandhi's initiative to mobilise indentured labour in South Africa and the textile labour in Ahmedabad coincided with his ideas of '*sarvodaya*' and trusteeship. The former had more radical underpinnings with his notion, borrowed from Ruskin, that all property is theft. He delineates how this radical notion gets transformed and his relation with industrial labour and indigenous business circles also changed over time is the subject of this paper. Gandhi's neglect of labour question has to be seen in the context of industrial labour class, which emerged in the second half of 19th century on the development of modern industries. However, the industrial labour in a predominantly agricultural country remained numerically small, but was concentrated in certain decisive centres with carry over of primordial pre-capitalist ethics and loyalties. Gandhi's method, considered workers as partners, and mill owners as trustees, a mere ploy to safeguard the interests of financiers of his movement? He contends that a critical interrogation of these aspects is essential to understand Gandhi.

Movva Srinivasa Reddy in his paper on 'Growth of Agro Industries in the Northern Circars' during the Inter-War Period (1919-39 AP)' discusses how industrial policy of British Government underwent change after World War I and how this shift in approach impacted native industry. He explains the mounting pressure from national movement and the need for economic balance in international markets on account of war-time compulsions, the British Government introduced some change in the industrial policies. They shifted from the policy of *laissez faire* to interventionist policies. Following these changes, we notice the development of modern industry. The colonial state attempts to develop industry by financial aid, tariff protection, commercial and industrial information, technical help, by demonstrating the use of better technology.

He argues on account of this state aid to industries, several native entrepreneurs – India, in general, and Andhra, in particular came forward to float industries. Loans were granted to entrepreneurs, shares were purchased, raw material was supplied to industries at concessional rates. Demonstration units and industrial schools were started with technical help.

His paper studies the nature of state aid to Industries Act, the rise of new entrepreneurial class, and the growth of agro industries in the Northern Circars of the present Andhra Pradesh and erstwhile Madras Presidency. It will be seen that agro-based industries such as sugar, jute, coir, oil milling, rice mills, were floated during the inter-war period.

The emergence of industrial labour as distinct social force and its deteriorating condition of life and work within and outside the industry were issues during colonial era. Manoj Kumar Sahoo in his paper on 'Emergence of Industry and Labour in Colonial Orissa' presents the development of industry and labour with initiative of native entrepreneurs. He explains how their efforts resulted in the growth of native industry in colonial Orissa. Orissa was famous for her industrial products in the pre-British period. In the early British rule, Orissa did not have heavy mechanised industries, except cottage, small scale and medium scale industries. These industries were the weaving textile industry, metal industry, rice industry, brass and bell metal industry, filigree industry, rope industry, paper industry, sugar industry, hide industry, silk weaving industry, paper industry, carpentry industry, fisheries, and so on. The products earned a good reputation not only in India but in other parts of the world, in general, and in European countries, in particular. It was the backbone of Orissa's economy and provided employment to the people of Orissa. In spite of foreign competition, the existence of industries had given Orissa some status in the field of industrial growth. Further, the formation of *Utkal Sammilani* in 1903 and the emergence of Madhusudan Das as pioneering industrialist played a formidable role in shaping the economic prosperity of Orissa. It took another shape with the formation of industrial department with separate Orissa province.

As far as labour in Orissa is concerned, we find three types of labour such as: agricultural, seasonal, semi-skilled and skilled labour. The standard of living was related to the social system. They were paid either in cash or kind. The semi-skilled and skilled labourers were mostly employed in weaving textile, handloom weaving, filigree industry, and so on. They were engaged in different industries by getting training. One of the interesting aspects of labour was the formation of trade union as leading organisation for ventilation of the industrial labourers' grievances in 1930s. The paper seeks to explore diverse aspects of industry and labour in colonial Orissa.

The industrial labour grew in opposition to colonialism of whatever hue and the capitalist class whether European or Indian offered determined resistance to the existence and continuation of colonial rule. The resistance of industrial labour against multiple forms of exploitation by colonial regime and capitalist masters has a tradition, beginning with the emergence of trade unions in the early twentieth century culminating with the revolt of RIN workers in British India of 1946. A. Suresh in his paper on 'Labour and the Anti-colonial Struggle in French India' focuses on the role of working class in anti-colonial struggle in French India. French India of five settlements and eleven *loges* comprise an area of little over 500 sq. kms, under French imperialism for more than two centuries. The native people lost their political, economic and socio-cultural rights and were subjected to the working class colonial exploitation. A strong labour movement was started in French India by early twentieth century, protecting and promoting class interests of industrial and agricultural labour. After lot of efforts and sacrifices on the part of the working class, the French colonial masters and the European capitalists relented and extended progressive labour rights to their colonies, which was considered something more progressive than the prevailing Asian standards. Soon, the working class clamoured for political independence from French colonial masters, who resorted to suppress the movement and weaken through encouraging division among nationalist elements. In the end, the French Indians succeeded in getting their territories transferred to the Indian Union. As such, the working class had played a significant role in the anti-colonial struggle against the French rule. His paper delineates the role played by working class in awakening political consciousness among French Indians and their contribution to anti-colonial struggle.

Bibin Kuriakose in his paper on "Working Class Resistance in Travancore: A Study of Punnapra Vayalar Struggle of 1946" discusses the contribution of working class in the state of Travancore. Before the formation of Kerala State in 1956, it was divided into three political units: Travancore, Cochin and Malabar. Apart from the directly ruled province of Malabar, the British exercised indirect control over the Princely States of Travancore and Cochin. This article explores the formation of working class in the erstwhile Travancore State and its subsequent involvement in the struggle for responsible government under the Communist Party with emphasis on Punnapra Vayalar Struggle of 1946. In the process, the paper traces the attitude of the Diwan of Travancore, Sir C.P. Ramaswamy Aiyer, who was very famous for his notoriety towards working class solidarity on class lines. It describes the conspicuous social and political situation in which the working class rose up in arms against the autocratic Diwan in 1946 and the active part in the freedom struggle. Except for a short period in 1942, the working class remained as militant group and supported the Travancore State Congress, but in the struggle against American Model Constitutional Reforms of 1946, it was the working class alone sacrificing against the State and the Diwan, resulting in the brutal killings of labourers. Instead of supporting the working class, the state Congress remained as a mere spectator, aloof from the Punnapra Vayalar struggle of 1946.

## References

1. **Note**: 'The economic geography of colonisation is as uneven as the geography of power', Frederick Cooper, 'Conflict and Connection: Rethinking Colonial African History', *The American Historical Review*, Vol. 99, No. 5. (Dec., 1994), p. 1529.
2. See for critical analysis of how colonial state is constituted in India redefining the power relations between the colonised and colonisers, Sabyasachi Bhattaacharya, 'Colonial Power and Micro-Social Interactions: Nineteenth Century India', *Economic and Political Weekly*, Vol. 26, No. 22/23 (June 1-8, 1991), pp. 1399-1403.
3. U. Kalpagam, 'Temporalities, History and Routines of Rule in Colonial India', *Time and Society*, 1999, Vol. 8 (1), p. 146.
4. *Ibid.,* p. 147.
5. *Ibid.,* p. 154.
6. *Ibid.,* p.154.

# 2

# World of Labour and Capital: Analysis of Gandhi's Political-Ideological Form, 1906-1934

*Shri Krishan*

## Introduction

The indigenous capital emerged slowly under the colonial rule despite domination of British capital in the key sectors of economy. Initially, the upper layers of the economy comprise big joint stock companies, managing agency houses, big banks and insurance companies, stock markets and foreign trade and shipping controlled by Britishers, while Indian merchant capital was retained in subordinate position as agents of foreign merchants or as usurers in new agrarian economy. The class-formation is never static and fixed despite structural constraints and indigenous capital, breaching 'collective monopoly' of British merchants and manufacturers through opportunities within the structure. The emergence of Indian indigenous capital class was partially linked to colonial structure and had the imprints of this relation. Armed with the legal protection and sanctity of contract, the Chettis of Tamil Nadu, the Konkani Saudagars, the Bohras and Parsis in Western India, and Marwari merchants of Sekhawati region in Rajasthan gradually entered industrial fields where variable production cost, due to cheap raw materials, was low.[1] However, economic criteria is not sufficient to determine and locate social class within the social division of labour.[2]

Similarly, the modern industrial labour in India emerged within the colonial economy, alongside mining, plantation, transport and manufacturing, especially the textile-production, both jute and cotton. This creates a new labour employment, entirely different from agricultural and artisan labour. This industrial force was drawn from rural hinterlands and migrated to urban centres like Kolkata and Mumbai. Though the nature of work, work place and life style changed for workers, the employment in industrial sector remained a temporary feature for quite a long period.[3] The workers stayed for some time in industrial employment and returned to villages for traditional loyalties of kinship, caste and religion. Did the rural migrants import a 'peasant-culture' into an urban setting? How the workers perceived their rural roots? According to Dipesh Chakrabarty, this 'peasant culture' was primarily, 'a pre-capitalist, inegalitarian culture marked by strong primordial loyalties of community, language, religion, caste and kinship.'[4] However, a simple notion of 'rural traditions' and 'peasant culture' poses problem because as Rajnarayan Chandavarkar points the agrarian society as being highly differentiated from within, and the traditions were varied and mostly small peasants migrated to the cities.[5] The urban neighbourhood were not, "repositories of primordial loyalties of working class. They provided materials from which wider class solidarities could be forged. Caste and kinship ties were vital to social organisation of workers; but so were the affinities of region and religion, workplace and neighbourhood, trade unions and political parties, cut across each other".[6]

Our concern here, is not to see the articulation of solidarity of class-location and position but precisely look at the fluidity and malleability. The 'proletariat' of colonies consists only in part of free wage earners as Marx conceived, i.e., "free in the double sense that as free individual he can dispose of his labour-power as his own commodity, and that, on the other hand, he has no other commodity for sale"[7]. In such peripheries, the majority of wage earners do not freely dispose of their labour power (for example, because they are burdened by debt) or they are not in a formal contractual relation with employers. Moreover, wage labour is integrated throughout in households and families whose survival always remains partly dependent on subsistence labour (performed chiefly, but not exclusively, by women), on the independent production of commodities for market. In many cases, the "roles" of various family members are not permanently fixed, but instead signify a transient social relationship which can be changed by other sources of income. We may thus conclude that the "authentic" working class is largely a fiction. The 'classical' proletariat is surrounded by, and intermingled with, a variegated 'semi-proletariat' of peddlers, sharecroppers, home workers, prostitutes, self-employed workers, beggars and scavengers. The boundaries between different segments are fluid, and finds expression in forms of organisation.

The focus on workers' politics and their place in local histories from a perspective of a 'history from below' is trendier. But, without an understanding of 'history from above', one cannot have a sense of what influences local responses. There are several possible ways of looking at the relation between Gandhi and indigenous capitalist class as well as labour. Initially, Gandhi was regarded as a 'bourgeois agent' who clothed his ideology in peasant populist clothes. He is seen as the leader of a mass formation which led a multi-class anti-imperialist democratic revolution in India. Some point high degree of ambiguity in Gandhi's relation to different social classes. Gandhi's synthesis of peasant millenarianism and 'bourgeois-rationality' has been evaluated differently. The subaltern studies collective highlighted the tensions and contestation between nationalism and 'subaltern' social groups and communities. However, still there is some scope for investigation of complexities of political-ideological forms evolved under the leadership of Gandhi, and ambiguities they represent. Gandhi's initiative to mobilise indenture labour in South Africa and the textile labour in Ahmedabad coincided with his ideas of '*sarvodaya*' and trusteeship. The former had more radical underpinning with his notion, borrowed from Ruskin that all property is theft. How this radical notion gets transformed and his relation with industrial labour and indigenous business circles change over time is the subject of this paper.

## Indentured Labour in South Africa

Gandhi's prolonged involvement in South African politics was confined to commercial social groups and opposition to Transvaal's immigration legislation to eliminate discrimination against Indians in principle. Gandhi describes the draft ordinance (Asiatic Laws Amendment Ordinance of 1906) as an attempt to lower the prestige of Indian community, where registration by mutual consent would have increased. It sought to 'humiliate not only ourselves but also the motherland'. He protests that he has "never known legislation of this nature being directed against free men in any part of the world". He knew that "indentured Indians in Natal are subject to a drastic system of passes, but these poor fellows can hardly be classed as freemen." Their oppression was anyway 'a mere fleabite' compared to the potential losses faced by wealthy traders, who could have faced with 'utter ruin in virtue of the Ordinance'.[8] (Emphasis added) Gandhi started to appeal directly to the underclass only in 1913 when he found that his *Satyagraha* is not making the desired impact. The repeal of the £ 3.0 tax on ex-indentured labour, which was added to movement's goals, extended his support base and allowed him to call a labour strike in Natal. Earlier, Gandhi was able to secure money for his movement from the wealthy Indians when H.S.L. Polak came to India for fund-raising. In November, 1909, Ratan Tata made first of several large donations to the Gandhian movement in South Africa. He contributed Rs. 25,000, to be followed by many more from other businessmen and over £ 8,000 was received during the next two years. Gandhi refused to be accountable to anyone in South Africa for disbursement of these funds. This money was used, in part, to keep Indian Opinion and the commune settlement at Phoenix running, paying off heavy debts incurred since Gandhi left his private legal practice which had helped finance both the paper and the settlement.[9]

## The Anti-Capitalist Ethics of *Sarvodaya*

Gandhi had already invented the moral weapon of *Satyagraha* which could be used tactically to mobilise unarmed cadres to obtain a specific limited political objective. He subsequently refined to breach the hegemony of the colonial state and make his own counter-hegemonic moves, using indigenous idioms and symbols. During his South African experiment, however, Gandhi also paraphrased Ruskin's *Unto the Last*[10] and evolved his notion of *Sarvodaya* from it. Gandhi constructed the theory of '*Sarvodaya*' based on Ruskin's ideas to counter the predominant mode of thinking of his times. Western capitalism breeds consumerism and accumulation of private capital. An individual remains as the centre of his political constructs, while questioning the economic individualism, on the level of political thought. Gandhi turns into a worst critic of capitalism.

He propounded a theory of social capital. He realised that individual labour creates capital, but capital has a social utility, endorsing the fact that the society has a right over capital. On the level of distribution, market should have a restricted role. Human consciousness has a role to play. Individuals, because of a higher level of consciousness and spiritual development, would allow the community to use their own property. Human initiative would not be lost at any point. Gandhi tried to reconstruct the concept of private property. One can have private property, but not for one's own use. It should be utilised for societal needs. That is why, individual needs have to be restricted to the minimum. This proposed restriction on human wants and needs upholds Gandhi different from present-day bio-economics dominated by managerial ethos and notions of resource-engineering. Gandhi believed that everybody could not be rich and that wealth at one pole was the result of deprivation at the other end. It was like the process of one bucket emptying out to fill the other bucket. The power of rupee one has possessed depended on another going without it. Wealth, according to him, was useless if it was not able to control the labour and lives of other people. Wealth and scarcity were, thus, the part of the same phenomenon. This fact was based on Gandhi's reading of John Ruskin. This is how Gandhi internalised and redefined Ruskin:

> "Political economy consists in the production, preservation and distribution, at the fittest time and place, of useful and pleasurable things.... Careful reflection will show that what we really desire through acquisition of wealth is power over other men—[power] to acquire for our advantage the labour of a servant, a tradesman or an artisan. And the power we can thus acquire will be in direct proportion to the poverty of others..... So that growing rich means contriving that as large a number of men as possible shall have less than we have. Economists generally assume that it is of advantage to the nation as a whole if the mass of people are thus kept in want. Equality among men is certainly not possible. But conditions of scarcity, unjustly created, injure the nation."[11]

Gandhi went to the extent of equating unlimited consumption and acquisition of wealth with that act of stealing. Gandhi further contends that economic and natural resources ought to be better managed in the service of common good. The equity in the distribution of resources is central in his thinking. Gandhi believed that the market forces were not capable of achieving this aim by themselves and, the market hence, has to be made subservient to societal needs. He cautioned against imitating the Western model of development, because it created the disease called wealth without work.

Gandhi compared the wealth to the flow of a river and stressed the regulation of its flow in his own inimitable style and use of peerless metaphors. Unfettered accumulation of wealth was unhealthy and to be avoided at all cost. He wrote:

> "Wealth is like a river. A river always flows towards the sea, that is, down an incline. So, as a general rule must wealth go where it is needed. But the flow of wealth, like the course of a river, can be regulated. Most of the rivers run out their courses unregulated, their marshy banks poisoning the wind. If dams are built across these rivers to direct the water flow as required, they will irrigate the soil and keep the atmosphere pure. Similarly, the uncontrolled use of wealth will multiply vices among men and cause starvation; in brief, such wealth will act like a poison. But the selfsame wealth, if its circulation is regulated and its use controlled, can, like a river whose stream has been properly harnessed, promote prosperity. The principle of regulating the circulation of wealth is ignored altogether by economists. Theirs is merely the science of getting rich."[12]

Gandhi discovered the profound and inherent connection between capitalism, colonialism, militarism and racialism and how they are about the exploitation of natural and human resources of the earth and advised like a first-rate teacher to develop an alternative value system. According to him, economists did not take men's conduct into account, but estimate prosperity from the amount of wealth accumulated and conclude that happiness of nations depends upon their wealth alone.

**The Labour Strikes in Natal**

Despite ideological underpinning of Gandhi's radical formulation, he moved to include the question of £ 3.0 tax only in September 1913 under political compulsions if one is to believe Maureen Swan. This has a huge potential to recruit thousands of indentured and ex-indentured labourers for a movement that remained confined to a few volunteers till this time. This was done when Gandhi's political leadership was under threat from the opponents of his policy in the Natal Indian Congress. The labour strike began on October 16, 1913 in the coal mines of Northern Natal. The move was hardly with any pre-planning and preparation, contrary to popular belief that Gandhi was the 'champion of indenture labourers' from mid-1890s and strike was a mere reflex response to Gandhi's initiative[13], Swan sees the strike as an example of spontaneous, unstructured and possessing a minimum support from the organisation and guided mainly by the 'traditional ideology' and popular culture.[14] In Northern Natal coal mines, some sort of rudimentary organisation, Tamil Benefit Society of Thambi Naidoo, played an important role and though there were other grievances of workers, the main economic grievance was imposition of £ 3.0 tax on Indian immigrants which Gandhi articulated at this stage. The economy already under the spell of depression, the tax made it difficult for the workers to freedom from indenture contract and many workers (about 65 per cent of the entire labour force, as Swan's estimate) were undergoing second and third terms of indenture. Government played a waiting game and did not intervene and break the strike. Gandhi responded by leading striking workers out of Natal that would culminate in illegal crossing over into Transvaal. It became imperative when the coalminers issued ultimatum to resume work, failing which they stop daily ration. Gandhi and the Natal Indian Association formed after split, found it difficult to maintain striking workers on minimal ration of bread and sugar, averaging around £ 250 a day. Funds were collected from sympathetic Indian merchants and £ 1,000 was received from India.[15] Gandhi estimated the shortfall in funds; despite contributions would be £ 6,000 per month.[16] However, the success of strike was ensured when it spread to sugar plantation of South Natal involving much workers. The crowd of workers portrayed a mythical leader in millenarian fashion with uncertainty of some outside leadership.[17] The workers on big plantation believed that a powerful rajah was going to pay them £ 3.0 not to work; on another they struck for fear that a rajah was coming to decapitate non-participant. One worker claimed that a Tamil handbill was circulated which announced that Gokhale was coming from India to abolish tax at once. It was even rumoured that Gokhale was coming with troops–as much as a regiment-with him. Some workers struck work because their neighbours had done so. Workers who knew Gandhi, and his connection with strike in the North, believed they were acting on his orders.[18] Compared to the North, there was more violence and tension in the South, but the event gave leverage for major concessions in 1914, especially the abolition of £ 3.0 tax on ex-indentured workers and right of a wife and minor children to join husbands in South Africa, even if it owed to polygamy. Other demands like movement of South Africa-born Indians to migrate from one province to another and a more just administration of laws affecting Indian commerce were not fulfilled in the compromise, but it raised the political status of Gandhi before his departure to India on July 18, 1914.

From the strikes of indentured workers, Gandhi learnt his basic political lesson: that mass action can paralyse the state and force it, if the action is non-violent, to its knees. If Government hit back, it would only lose its moral legitimacy before the people.

**The Ahmedabad Labour Struggle**

Although Gandhi's *Satyagraha* in India followed broad pattern of those in South Africa, as we shall see later, he also introduced several changes to suit new and needs and circumstances. The idea of fasting became the subject of much debate throughout life. For reasons to be discussed later, Gandhi had no doubt whatsoever that a fast was not a hunger-strike, nor a form of moral or emotional blackmail, nor a way of evoking and exploiting others' pity, but a form of self-sacrifice and a perfectly moral method of action. His past experiences had convinced him that human actions sprang from 'both the head and the heart', and that a community could not be shaken out of its complacency on issues of vital and moral importance by sermons and arguments alone. One had to touch people's hearts and activate their consciences, and fasting was one of the most effective ways to do so. As Gandhi understood its nature and mechanism, it was derived from two distinct ideas, the Hindu idea of *tapas* (penance) and the predominantly Christian idea of suffering. The fast was an attempt to purify oneself, to generate moral energy from within and mobilise the moral energies of intended constituency.

Gandhi's symbols did not appeal to emotions alone, for he also offered elaborate rational arguments in their defence; neither were they simply mystical or transcendental, for they were all drawn from the daily lives of ordinary Indians. They appealed to the head and the heart, interests and cultural memories, the present and the past, and were designed to reach out to the 'whole being' of his countrymen and mobilise their moral energies.

The textile workers of Ahmedabad started a strike in 1918 with a demand for increasing wages. Anusuyaben Sarabhai had begun social work among mill workers in Ahmedabad, an activity which lead to the founding of the famous Mazdoor Mahajan—Textile Labour Association, in 1920. Gandhi declared that the Textile Labour Association, Ahmedabad, was his laboratory for experimenting with his ideas on industrial relations and a model labour union. He was duly satisfied with the success of the experiment and advised other trade unions to emulate. As the mill owners opposed their demands, Mahatma Gandhi started a hunger strike and, as a result, the strike was settled. According to the settlement, the wages of workers were increased by 35 percent. There were reasons for the spurt in unions. Prices had soared following the World War I. Wages had not kept pace with the inflation. The mill-owners' attempt to end the 'plague bonus' of 1917 led to confrontation despite attempt of Gandhi to mediate. Initially, workers demand a 50 per cent increase in wage which was scaled down to 35 per cent after Gandhi's advice. Gandhi now has to deal with the indigenous capitalist class in Ahmedabad while the strike of indentured labour in South Africa was against the state. The ideological and political form and his tactics of intervention also changed. In a speech to striking mill-hands of Ahmedabad on February 8, 1918, Gandhi advised them to shed bitterness and make use of the method of arbitration.[19] Gandhi's new approach, which came to be known as 'trusteeship', was well articulated in a series of leaflets during the textile workers' strike in early 1918. As Gandhi had novel ideas about political goal and method, he had his own ideas about the capital-labour relationship[20].

He considered the workers as partners, working for public good, and mill owners as their trustees. Any quarrel in between be settled through mutually agreed arbitration. He also laid down the functions of the trade unions in his own way. His conception of trade union work was that they were not merely to agitate for rights and organise strikes but to work for social advancement of labourers and their families. For this purpose, he placed schemes of constructive work such as organisation of crèches, day schools for their children, night classes for adults, enforcement of prohibition before the labour organisations. The Ahmedabad Textile Labour Association, locally known as Mazdoor Mahajan, founded in 1918, distinctly reflected Gandhian thoughts on labour, employer-employee' relation and the method of tackling.[21] In the leaflet Number 6, issued during the strike, Gandhi enunciated these views in the familiar terms. He wrote:

> "Pure justice is that which is inspired by fellow-feelings and compassion. We in India call it the eastern or the ancient way of justice. That way of justice, which has no place in it for the fellow feeling or compassion, is known as satanic, Western or modern justice. Out of compassion or regard, son and father concede many things to each other to the eventual benefit of both........There was a time in India when

servants, passing from father to son, used to serve in the same family for generations. They were regarded and treated as the members of the family."[22]

Once Gandhi reduced the labour-capital struggle to familial domain, it became easier to distance it from the 'class-struggle' perspective. He reminded Ahmedabad workers how white workers employed in railways had struck work, when Indian workers' strike was suspended because our aim was not to dislodge Government.[23] Gandhi introduced a few key concepts in the struggle, like the idea of dignity of labour. In the leaflet number 11, issued during the strike, Gandhi remarked that "A worker's capital is inexhaustible, incapable of being stolen, and bound to pay him a generous dividend all the time. His hands and feet, the energy which enables him to work, constitutes this inexhaustible capital of his and the wages constitutes his dividends."[24] In the leaflet No. 14, Gandhi invested in labour struggle the 'erotic and moral energies' by uttering these words: "The struggle is not merely for a 35 per cent increase; it is to show that the workers are prepared to suffer for their rights. We are fighting to withhold our honour. We have launched this struggle to better ourselves......Farhad broke stones for the sake of Shirin, his beloved. For the workers, their pledge is their Shirin. Why not break stones for its sake? For the sake of truth, Harishchandra sold himself; why should workers not suffer hardships for upholding their pledge? For the sake of their honour, Imam Hasan and Hussain suffered greatly. Should we not be prepared even to die for our honour?"[25] Gandhi resorted to fasting to keep the morale of the workers high and to demonstrate his resolve for renunciation and sharing their suffering when some workers felt that Gandhi was moving in car with Anasuyabehn (the sister of Gandhi's capitalist benefactor Ambalal Sarabhai who had contributed Rs. 13,000 to his Ashram secretly when other sources of donations to Ashram dried after Gandhi's insistence to allow entry of 'untouchables' in his Ashram) and probably having sumptuous meals. Gandhi describes the circumstances which forced him to fast. Finally, a wage hike of 35 per cent was achieved after this fast and strike.[26]

**After the Ahmedabad Fast**

Gandhi did not take part directly in any other struggle after the successful completion of his objective in Ahmedabad, but he continued to express his views on labour problems, advised them whenever he had an opportunity. In a speech to the Tramways workers at Madras, he justified workers' call to strike in case their grievances were legitimate and their employers were not willing to redress them.[27] In an article in *Navajivan* (Gandhi's Gujarati paper), written on 8th February, 1920, Gandhi said that in the struggle between capital and labour, mostly the capitalists are at fault but if labour is conscious of its numerical strength, it can also become tyrannical. In such cases, if the labour starts dictating terms to capitalist, it would harm the industries of the country. Narrating how the employers try to get maximum service from labourers with minimum payment and equally how the workers make use of tricks to get maximum payment with minimum work, Gandhi advised them to behave as 'members of one and the same family.' Summing up his position on capital-labour relation, Gandhi wrote: "Strikes, cessation of work and *hartals* are wonderful things, no doubt, but it is not difficult to abuse them. Workmen ought to organise themselves into strong labour unions, and on no account shall they strike work without the consent of these unions. Strikes should not be risked without the previous negotiations with the mill-owners. If mill-owners resort to arbitration, the principle of *panchayats* should be accepted. And once the *panch* are appointed, their decisions must be accepted by both the parties alike, whether they like it or not."[28]

Gandhi, who generally favoured equality of men and women in many fields, but stressed the ideology of domesticity, predicted on a gradual differentiation of the roles of men and women, a dissociation of production and consumption, the economy and the family. According to Samita Sen, "The ideological valourisation of 'domestic' was not merely a matter of marking out an autonomous domain where the 'nation' was to be located. It was also a part of larger social movement whereby the confirmation and maintenance of elite status became increasingly dependent on a sharply enunciated separated between domesticity and productivity, locating men in the first and women in the latter."[29] In a speech at the meeting of mill-hands of Ahmedabad on February, 25, 1920, Gandhi advocated that women should not work in the factories:

> "They have plenty of work in their own homes. They should attend to the bringing up of their children; they must give peace to their husbands when he returns home tired, administer to him, soothe him if he is angry, and do any other work they can staying at home. If we want our family life to be comely and sweet, we ought to do this.

> It is not for women to go out and work, as men do. If we send them to factories, who will look after our domestic and social affairs? If women go out to work, our social life will be ruined and moral standards will decline."[30]

Gandhi condemned the employment of child labour in mills because 'no nation worthy of name can possibly afford so to misuse her children' and stressed the need for reduction of working hours for the labour in general, but simultaneously wished that women should be weaned away from working in the mills. Gandhi comments: "if man and woman are partners in life and complementary to each other, they become good householders only by dividing their labour, and a wise mother finds time fully occupied in looking after her household and children. But where both husband and wife have to labour for mere maintenance, the nation must become degraded. It is like a bankrupt living on his capital."[31] On the positive side, Gandhi had learnt from his experience that organisation of prolonged strikes is a costly affair. He advised the labourers that strikes should be self-supporting and should not depend on unions for sustenance during the periods of strikes. To quote his words: "The labourers looked at pecuniary support from their unions for the maintenance. No labour can prolong a strike indefinitely so long as labour depends upon the resources of its union. So strike can absolutely succeed but cannot be indefinitely prolonged. In all strikes that I have conducted, I have laid down one indispensable rule, that labourers must find their own support."[32] Regarding formation of an all-India organisation of trade union and affiliation of Ahmedabad union with that in

1927, Gandhi lamented the fragmentation of labour as a class. Writing to Shapurji Saklatvala, he remarked:

> "Labour in India is still extremely unorganised. The labourers have no mind of their own, when it comes to matters of national policy or the general welfare of labour itself. Labourers in various parts of India have no social contact and no other mutual ties. It is provincial and even in the same city it is highly communal. It is not everywhere wisely guided. In many places, it is under selfish and highly unscrupulous guidance. There is no absolute cohesion amongst provincial labour leaders, and there is little discipline among sub-leaders. The latter do not uniformly tender obedience to their provincial chiefs. Leaders in different provinces have no single policy to follow. In these circumstances, an all-India union can only exist on paper. I hold it to be suicidal therefore for Ahmedabad to think of belonging to it."[33]

Gandhi again intervened in a labour dispute between textile labourers in Ahmedabad and the industrialists in early 1929 because the workers were demanding restoration of wages to the extent of 15.5 per cent done by mill-owners in 1923, but when Gandhi and industrialist Mangaldas Girdharidas failed to settle as *panch*, the third party arbitrator, Dewan Bahadur Krishnalal Mohanlal Zaveri was asked to give a verdict. Gandhi disagreed with the judgement of Zaveri on the ground that their living wage was less with a actual cost of living, had not urged for a restoration of wages even at the level of 1923. Gandhi forcefully argued the case of workers and cited empirical evidence to support for restoration of wage but accepted the verdict given by Zaveri.[34] Gandhi enunciated a fundamental principle at this juncture. He said: "In my opinion, any amount that has to be withdrawn from the capital should be regarded as a loss. No loss is incurred if there is less profit. A fall in profit should never be a reason for decrease in labourers' wages."[35] (Emphasis added)

**Gandhi's Relations with the Capitalists**

The anti-capitalist underpinnings of *Sarvodaya* ideology which Gandhi articulated in South Africa, however, weakened when the task was to lead labourers against the indigenous capitalist class. Gandhi's identification with labour did not conflict with his friendship with capital. He has ranged against capitalists in Ahmedabad in 1918 but was also regularly getting financial support and backing for his various endeavours from the capitalists, notably from Sarabhai, Birla, Tata, Bajaj, Godrej and many others.[36] The notion of trusteeship had hardly as radical potential as the earlier *Sarvodaya* concept had. Gandhi's ideal was that capital and labour should supplement and help each other. In his words: "They should be a great family living in unity and harmony, capital not only looking to the material welfare of labourers but their material welfare also, capitalist being trustees for the welfare of the labouring classes under them."[37] According to Aditya Mukherjee, Indian capitalist class favoured the constitutional path and feared mass civil disobedience as that could threaten capitalism and harmed its business. However, in his view, the dominant section of this capitalist class started supporting the Indian National Congress, but it never was in a position to dominate the movement.[38] Claude Markovits, on the other hand, feels that there was no uniformity in the relationship between Indian businessmen and Congress, which was uneasy and changing during the period of political turmoil and realignment in 1930s.[39] It seems whatever suspicions and misgivings the capitalists might have, they were dispelled by the use of familial discourses by Gandhi in describing the relationship between capitalists with their workers. This is what Gandhi said about Bajaj's relationship with his labourers:

> "Jamnalalji knows in his heart no distinction between a *seth* and a servant, and his shop-assistants, cooks, coachmen and other servants are treated as members of the family. He knows that they need leisure as he needs it, he knows that they need a holiday occasionally as he needs it (but rarely takes it), he knows that they need to live with their wives and children in fair comfort.....And he knows the wretched lot of the average shop-assistant, sweating for ten to thirteen hours without a holiday, on a miserable salary, having to go on leave, if he can get it, without pay, losing every day in health, living a life without cheer, an eternal grind from morning till night."[40]

Gandhi's relation with some capitalists were so intimate that he even indulged in guiding them into his pet business projects. For instance, he urged G.D. Birla to buy a tannery owned by Madhusudan Das in Cuttack in the interest of cow-protection on the following three conditions, 1. Only hides of dead animals will be taken, 2. The practice of killing *patlaghos* (kind of iguana) for the sake of their hides must be discontinued, 3. The idea of charging interest must be given up; if there is any profit, it should be used for the expansion of the tannery.[41] In another case, Gandhi disapproved of purchase of a cotton textile mill by Jamnalal Bajaj which Bajaj's friends and business associate had persuaded him to buy so that the interests of mill-workers can be taken care of in accordance with Gandhi's wishes and at the same time making a reasonable profit.[42] The ambivalent positioning of Gandhi comes openly in a letter written to Ranchodlal on September 14, 1929. Gandhi felt that the argument that workers are entitled to a higher wage only if they reformed themselves is like laying a condition that we can get Swaraj only if we reformed ourselves. Gandhi rather advocated that workers are entitled to an enough 'subsistence' wage. If not, they must get more. He also favoured establishment of 'ideal' mills by the 'enlightened' mill owners. He wrote: "It will take ages for our workers to be able to run an ideal mill. Why do you think it is futile to hope that an unselfish capitalist may set up an ideal mill. Cadbury has opened an ideal factory. Lever brothers have built an ideal settlement for their workers. Some such effort has also been definitely made by Narottamdas at Sholapur. Tata certainly laid a foundation of such a settlement at Jamshedpur."[43]

Gandhi's philosophy, particularly in regard to economics, was not a ready-made answer to the economic needs of the Indian capitalist class. His conception of Hind Swaraj, properly realised, left no role for capitalists. The modern western industrial society, which rested on private property, profit and a Machiavellian notion of power, did not appeal to Gandhi. To acquire, to have and to multiply wealth were considered sacred and unalienable right in the capitalist acquisitive society.[44] To oppose this, Gandhi made use of the ancient Indian notion of '*Aparigraha*' or non-possession of unnecessary material goods.[45] Gandhi went to the extent of equating unlimited consumption and acquisition of wealth similar to the acts of stealing. To quote him again:

> "If I take anything that I do not need for my immediate use, and keep it, I thieve it from somebody else. I venture to suggest that it is the fundamental law of nature, without exception, that nature produces enough for our wants from day-to-day, and if only everybody took enough for himself and nothing more, there would be no pauperism in the world, there would be no starvation in the world. But so long as we have got this inequality, so long we are thieving..."[46]

Gandhi was seeking the conversion of capitalists, not their destruction. He felt that inequalities of wealth are natural and only solution was a co-sharing of this wealth. The following passage sums up his position quite beautifully:

"Inequalities in intelligence and even opportunities will last till the end of time. A man living on the bank of river has any day more opportunities of growing crops than one living in an arid desert. But if inequalities stare us in the face the essential equality too is not to be missed. Every man has an equal right to the necessaries of life even as birds and beasts have......And if I would recognise the fundamental equality, as I must, of the capitalist and the labourers, I must not aim at his destruction. I must strive for his conversion."[47]

Gandhi believed that if capitalist could be purged of their selfishness and start sub-serving the interests of the poor, the unbridgeable gulf that existed between the 'haves' and 'have-nots' could be reduced and class-divisions there will be, but they would be then horizontal, not vertical. Such a system would be like reformed *varnashrama* and act as means of harmonising difference between high and low, as well as between capital and labour. His advice to the radical students was not to imitate Western models. In his words: "Lets study our Eastern institutions in that spirit of scientific enquiry and we shall evolve a truer communism that the world has yet dreamed of. It is surely wrong to presume that Western Socialism or Communism is the last word on the question of mass poverty."[48] He further clarified his position in a statement made in 1934 regarding the relation between nationalist goal of *Swaraj* and social restructuring as follows:

> "Two things—the social re-ordering and the fight for political swaraj—must go hand in hand. There can be no question of precedence or division into water-tight compartments here. But a new social order cannot be 'forced'; that would be remedy worse than the disease. I am an impatient reformer. I'm for all through-going, radical, social-re-ordering but it must be an organic growth, not a violent super-imposition."[49] (Emphasis added)

Thus, one element in Gandhi's philosophy, trusteeship, led to the breakup of capitalist concentration of business and industry into units of agriculture and cottage industry. The process of nationalism and big-business interpenetration started in right earnest. Gandhi's notion of trusteeship was able to achieve a kind of 'vertical integration' of antagonistic class interests of workers and capitalists, enabling his movement to cut across such distinctions by portraying them as members of a single family. Gandhi, in this endeavour, was not attempting to assimilate and develop European cultural and political forms. But his fetishisation of paternal familial forms, as ideal, artificially freezes the cultural difference. Gandhi could, thus, direct popular forces and thereby gain hegemony over them by providing some space for workers practices and politics. However, the workers practices and politics could not be synchronous with the nationalist project of state-formation; they had their own histories and trajectories. As pure and abstract political 'subjects' exist only on paper, in reality, the workers could find themselves embedded in pre-capitalist cultural and political forms. Gandhi's idea of suffering, renunciation, daily *yajna* (for any nationalist cause), *tapascharya*, and capitalists as paternal figures embedded in a modern matrix of just social order or *ramrajya*[50], equality and fraternity was a heady mixture that easily appealed to the mill-hands as well as the other toilers. Furthermore, the study of Gandhi's political-ideological forms reveals that there need not be a correspondence between economic, cultural and political forms.

## References

1. Thomas A. Timberg, *The Marwaris, From Traders to Industrialists*, Vikas Publishing House, New Delhi, 1978 traces this evolution in the case of *Marwaris*. Also see V. I. Pavlov, *Indian Capitalist Class: A Historical Study*, People's Publishing House, New Delhi, 1964.
2. Poulantzas, Nicos, "On Social Classes" in A. Giddens and D. Held (eds.), *Classes, Power and Conflict*, Berkeley: California University Press, 1982, pp. 101-12.
3. Morris D. Morris, *The Emergence of an Industrial Labour Force in India: A Study of Bombay Cotton Mills*, 1854-1947,

Berkeley and Los Angeles, 1965 was first pioneering work to point out this. Also see Ranajit Das Gupta, "Factory labour in Eastern India: Source of Supply, 1855-1946: Some Preliminary Findings" *Indian Economic and Social History Review*, Vol. 13(3), 1976, pp. 277-328.

4. Dipesh Chakrabarty, *Re-thinking Working Class History: Bengal, 1890-1940*, Princeton University Press, Princeton, 1989.
5. Rajnarayan Chandavarkar, " 'The Making of Working Class': E. P. Thompson and Indian History", in Vinayak Chaturvedi, ed., *Mapping Subaltern Studies and The Post-Colonial*, Verso, London and New York, 2000, pp. 50-71.
6. *Ibid*, p. 61.
7. Karl Marx, *Capital*, Vol. I, trans. Ben Fowkes (Harmondsworth: Penguin, 1976), p. 272.
8. M.K. Gandhi, 'Satyagraha in South Africa,' in S. Narayan, ed., *Selected Works of Mahatma Gandhi*, Navajivan Publishing House, Ahmedabad, 1968, Vol. III, pp. 137-38.
9. Maureen Swan, *Gandhi: The South African Experience*, Ravan Press, Johannesburg, 1985, pp. 225-26.
10. John Ruskin (1819-1900) was a Scotsman and author of many books on architecture, painting and social problems of industrial society. He was Slade Professor of Art in Oxford for some time. He was opposed to vivisection of animals for experiments, opposed usury and was also interested in worker's education and cooperative industrial settlements. His social utopia influenced Gandhi in South Africa. In Gandhi's own words Ruskin was "one of the three modern scholars...who made a deep impression on me". Reading *Unto the Last* "brought about an instantaneous and practical transformation...I rose with dawn, ready to reduce these principles to practice." See Gandhi, *Autobiography*, Part IV, Ch. XVIII.
11. *Indian Opinion*, 13/06/1908 , Gandhi, *Collected Works*, Vol. VIII: 368-69.

12. *Sarvodaya*, VIII, Indian Opinion, 4/7/1908, Gandhi, *Collected Works*, Vol. VIII: 419-21.
13. Louis Fischer, *The Life of Mahatma Gandhi*, Harper, 1950, p. 63& 126.
14. Swan, *Gandhi: The South African Experience*, p. 246.
15. Swan, *Gandhi: The South African Experience*, pp. 247-51.
16. Gandhi, *Collected Works*, Vol. XII, (Govt. of India, New Delhi) Gandhi to Gokhale, before 6 Nov. 1913.
17. See Shahid Amin, "Gandhi as Mahatma", in Ranajit Guha ed., *Subaltern Studies*, Vol. III, Oxford University Press, New Delhi, 1984, pp. for how peasants perceived Gandhi in another context.
18. Swan, *Gandhi: The South African Experience*, pp. 251-52.
19. Gandhi, *Collected Works*, Vol. XI, p. 248.
20. See Kripalani, J.B. *Gandhi: His Life and Thought*. New Delhi: Publications Division, Ministry of Information and Broadcasting, 1975.
21. See Gandhi, M.K., *An Autobiography or The Story of My Experiments with Truth*, translated from Gujarati by Mahadev Desai. London: Phoenix Press, 1949.
22. Gandhi, *Collected Works*, Vol. XI, pp. 302-03.
23. Gandhi, *Collected Works*, Vol. XI, pp. 306-07.
24. Gandhi, *Collected Works*, Vol. XI, p. 325.
25. Gandhi, *Collected Works*, Vol. XI, p. 333.
26. Gandhi, *Collected Works*, Vol. XI, p. 335-36 and also see Eric. H. Erikson, *Gandhi's truth: on the origins of militant nonviolence*, Norton Publishers, 1969 for a detailed study of this strike and Gandhi's relation with Sarabhai family.
27. Gandhi, *Collected Works*, Vol. XVII, p. 342.
28. Gandhi, *Collected Works*, Vol. XIX, (from *Navajivan*, 8-02-1920) p. 388.
29. Samita Sen, *Women and Labour in late Colonial India: The Bengal Jute Industry*, Cambridge University Press, Cambridge, 1999, p. 60.

30. Gandhi, Speech at Meeting of mill-hands, Ahmedabad, April, 18, 1920 in *Collected Works*, Vol. XIX, p. 422.
31. Gandhi, *Collected Works*, Vol. XX, p. 220, (From *Young India*, 28-04-1920 and 5-05-1920).
32. Gandhi, *Collected Works*, Vol. XXI, p. 169.
33. Gandhi, *Collected Works*, Vol. XXXVIII, pp. 361-62 (Letter to Shapurji Saklatvala, Nandi Hills (Mysore State), May 10, 1927.
34. Reference for this is from Gandhi, *Collected Works*, Vol. XLVII and XLVIII.
35. Gandhi, *Collected Works*, Vol. XLIII, p. 89.
36. There are many instances of financial help from these businessmen to Gandhi's causes. Jamnalal Bajaj contributed Rs 2 lakhs for supporting the families of lawyers who gave up practice at the call of Non-Cooperation. This fund was later merged with Tilak Swaraj Fund. Bajaj also contributed Rs. 2, 50, 000 to Gandhi Sewa Sangh (1923) with the object of creating volunteers for service to the country. For All-India-Khaddar Board, Gandhi wrote in *Harijan*: "I may have given the mantra, but Jamnalalji devoted his intelligence, his power of organisation and his money to give shape to the scheme." (*Harijan*, 8-03-1942) There was some more financial contribution from Bajaj. The spacious Garden House in Wardha which housed All-India Village Industries Association (1935) was gifted by him. Navajivan Publication in Hindi was also entirely financed by Bajaj and so was the establishment of Sewagram Ashram in Wardha after Gandhi took a pledge not to return to Sabaramti Ashram till Swaraj was attained during the Dandi March. See Kaka Kalelkar, ed., *To A Gandhian Capitalist: Correspondence between Mahatma Gandhi and Jamna Lal Bajaj and Members of his family*, Sevak Prakashan, Bombay, 1951, pp. 33-44.
37. Gandhi, *Collected Works*, Vol. XXXII, p. 271 (From *Young India*, 20-08-1925).
38. Aditya Mukherjee, "Indian Capitalists and the Nationalist Movement" in Bipan Chandra and Mridula Mukherjee, eds.,

*India's Struggle for Independence*, Penguin Books (India) Ltd., 1988, pp. 378-81. This thesis has been elaborated more fully in his latest work on this theme, *Imperialism, Natioanlism and Making of the Indian capitalist Class, 1920-47*, Sage Publications, Delhi, 2003.

39. Aditya Mukherjee, "Indian Capitalists and the Nationalist Movement" in Bipan Chandra and Mridula Mukherjee, eds., *India's Struggle for Independence*, Penguin Books (India) Ltd., 1988, pp. 378-81. This thesis has been elaborated more fully in his latest work on this theme, *Imperialism, Natioanlism and Making of the Indian capitalist Class, 1920-1947*, Sage Publications, Delhi, 2003.
40. Kaka Kalelkar, ed., *To A Gandhian Capitalist*, pp. 52-53 (Quoted from *Harijan*, 23-10-1937).
41. Gandhi, *Collected Works,* Vol. XXXIII, pp. 15-16 (Letter to G. D. Birla, Patna, September 27, 1925).
42. Kaka Kalelkar, ed., *To A Gandhian Capitalist*, p. 117.
43. Gandhi, *Collected Works*, Vol. XLVII, pp. 69-70 (Letter to Ranchodlal, September, 14, 1929).
44. Tawney R. H. (1920): *The Acquisitive Society,* New York : Harcourt Brace.
45. The term *aparigrah* is just the opposite of *parigrah* which means 'to amass', 'to accumulate', 'to compile', 'to seize', 'to hold', and 'to receive or accept gifts'. It is defined as that which entangles one from all sides. (*Parigahanam Parigraha*) *Parigraha* has two implications according to Jainas (i) *Bahya* (outer) meaning worldly possessions (ii) *Abhyantara* (inner) meaning attachment. Both these implications together refer to an attitude of mind towards material objects. These are not two kinds of *parigraha* but are actually two components of *parigraha. Parigraha* thus means not only possessions, but also possessiveness.
46. Speech on 'Ashram Vows' at YMCA, Madras, *The Indian Review*, February, 1916. Quoted in Weber, Thomas (2004): *Gandhi as Disciple and Mentor* (Cambridge and New York: Cambridge University Press), p. 210.

47. Gandhi, *Collected Works*, Vol. LI, p. 296.
48. Gandhi, *Collected Works*, Vol. LXIV, p. 204.
49. Gandhi, *Collected Works*, Vol. LXIV, p. 205.
50. N.D. Irani and Silver Morris, eds., *Social Justice in Ancient World*, Greenwood Press, Westport, 1995, shows that every society had its ideas about social justice but also a notion of proper social hierarchy and rules to be observed to maintain it.

# 3

# Growth of Agro Industries in the Northern Circars (1919-1939)

*Movva Srinivasa Reddy*

## Introduction

The process of deindustrialisation in India, which started in the 18th century, continued till the second half of the 19th century. We notice the growth of modern Indian industry from the middle of the 19th century. However, the process of industrialisation and the British industrial policy in India did not have virtues of a healthy growth till the end of the First World War. It was only during the inter-war period that we see a real change in industrial policy. We observe the growth of modern industry in India. An attempt is being made in this paper to study this growth in the Northern Circars during the inter-war period. Here the growth of agro industries alone is examined.

## Industrial Policies Pre-World War-I

Basing on the doctrine of laissez-faire, the British rulers held the government as ill-qualified for any development by direct action, and that matters be left to private enterprises. Hence, the state assistance before

1919, was meagre and took two forms: (1) wholly inadequate provision of technical education; and (2) half-hearted attempt of commercial and industrial information[1]. The few British officials like Curzon at the centre and Chatterton at the Madras Presidency tried to play a positive role for developing industry, but their policy suffered opposition from business interests at London and British administrators in India, guided by laissez-faire policies.

## Change in Industrial Policies Post-World War-I

The First World War created favourable conditions for India, declining British industries, to face emerging industrial powers like U.S.A. and Japan. Britain was surpassed by U.S.A. and Germany by the early 1890s, in the production of steel. British cotton textiles lost competitive power and relied for markets mainly on its colonies. Britain, as Hobsbawn observed, "was becoming a parasitic rather than a competitive economy"[2]. The economy of the first industrial power in the world began to decline because of its conservatism, and its technology was archaic, unlike its rivals U.S.A. It failed to adopt mass production methods and cartels and monopolies were slow to develop here[3]. Beside the economic reasons, global strategic considerations played an important role. The First World War highlighted the necessity of an industrial base in the East for the conduct of a modern war. Under these circumstances, the Indian Industrial Commission was appointed in May 1916 to report upon the possibilities of further industrial development.

## Indian Industrial Commission's Recommendations (1918)

The Commission recommended Indian industries be largely based on agricultural products and its services require strengthening on sustainable research. It felt the system of state technical education and scholarship for studing abroad could students acquire training in new industries. They recommended opening of more technical schools and depend on the advice from the commercial and to industrial intelligence department at the Centre and provinces for overseas trade answering queries from the public. The Commission also recommended direct technical assistance for certain industries, in the form of loans to agricultural and industrial societies for purchase and employment and buy costly machinery and plant[4]. The Commission expressed supporting the policies of protectionism for developing more industries.

**Protection to Indian Industries**

In the year 1924, the interests of iron and steel industry and later, the paper industry were safeguarded. In 1927, and in subsequent years, with similar safeguarding. Cotton textiles industry, an infant industry suffered unfair competition from Japan. The sugar industry got adequete support in 1932.[5]

In the year 1920, the Secretary of State in a dispatch, instructed the Government to play an active role in the industrial development at the cost of administrative equipment armed with reliable scientific and technical advice.

**New Industrial Policy in the Madras Presidency**

On 15th March 1920, the Government of Madras Presidency convened a conference where appreciable number of commercial and industrial interests as well as the member of the legislative council took part. Board of Industries was created in the Presidency with five divisions headquartered at Bezawada, Bellary,

Coimbatore, Madura and Madras. Bezawada Division with which we deal in this paper had the following districts under its jurisdiction: Ganjam, Visakhapatnam, Godavari, Guntur and Krishna districts. Each division was placed under the supervision of an Assistant Director. His duties were collection and dissemination of commercial and industrial intelligence, the supervision of industrial and weaving parties within their jurisdiction, local investigations, and enquiries in connection with industries to take advantage of the facilities offered by the department[6].

## Industries in the Northern Circars

The Northern Circars roughly corresponds to the present districts of Srikakulam, Vizianagaram, Visakhapatnam, East and West Godavari, Krishna and Guntur in the State of Andhra Pradesh. Textile and handloom industries flourish while Machilipatnam served as the chief trading centre of ships to many parts of the world.[7]

A host of commodities, especially several varieties of textiles from Machilipatnam, found their way to Timor, Ambojia, Mouluccas, Patni, Bantam, Batavia, Jambi, Achin, Bnada and Siam. Among the textile products exported from Machilipatnam to these markets of South East Asia were Golconda cloth, Guinea cloth, Madops, Salampuries, Gingams, Sarassas, Beetilles, Paroallas, Gulangs and Tapis[8].

## Deindustrialisation

We find the region of Northern Circars flourished in textile industry before Europe's industrialisation. The import of Western textiles started. The export of piece goods registered a sharp decline. In the Godavari district in a quinquenium in 1821-25, piece goods worth Rs. 8.68 lakh were annually exported. The annual value of exports declined to a mere Rs. 2.01 lakh between 1845-49.[9]

**Economic Transformation**

By an agreement between the British and the Nizam in 1766, the latter granted the five Circars as a free gift to the Company. The Company introduced the permanent settlement during 1802-04. This increased the forces of exploitation. Seasons were unfavourable with depression in agricultural prices and decline in cropped area. The conditions made cultivation an unprofitable profession during the first half of the 19th century[10].

Some anicuts were built across the rivers Godavari and Krishna in 1850-60. Irrigation injected forces of dynamism into the agrarian economy. We see the process of commercialisation of agriculture setting in this region, following dam construction.

**Commercialisation of Agriculture**

The period of nearly two decades from 1877-78 onwards, the total cropped area in the Krishna district increased significantly from over 18 lakh acres to 23 lakh acres[11]. The non-food crops enlarged their share of total cultivated area. Among the non-food crops, cotton, which was one of the cash crops registered significant decline, in terms of area and share in total land under cultivation. The share of food crops fell to by about 4 per cent, but rice increasingly became a major crop, occupying well over 1/5th of the total cropped area. The share of rice in total cropped area rose from 1/4th in 1870 to 1/3rd in 1890s making way for food surplus[12].

In the Godavari district, paddy and oil seeds were grown on commercial lines, in the belifes that sugarcane cultivation would get into commercial dimensions, owing to expenditure being relatively high compared to paddy. Nata Duvvury has shown that tobacco was being cultivated on commercial lines in the Guntur district from 1920s onwards[13].

**Emergence of Entrepreneurial Class**

Commercialisation of agriculture led to food surplus in the commodity market for agricultural products, across Vijayawada, Guntur and Kakinada. The introduction of Ryotwari system promoted production for market confirming the ownership rights on land. Economic changes attracted relatively large class of prosperous peasants or owner cultivators. The newly rich peasant cultivators began to participate in the market, as sellers, buyers and traders with higher productivity. The big farmers were able to accumulate substantial surpluses from agriculture looked more profitable ways to invest their savings[14].

These savings were started to be invested in purchase of additional land. However, there is a limit beyond which the land cannot be cultivated profitably. Hence, the rich landlords started buying unoccupied lands from the Government, influencing revenue officials, in procuring water and in turn sell the land. Such lands were found exhausted by early 1920s, making the Ryots turn to money lending. This avenue was also closed following Co-operative Banks lending at lower rates. As a result, the newly rich Delta Ryots began to look for other investment opportunities. Some entered into grain trade, buying paddy on commission and transporting it to the mills. About 12 Ryots in each of the villages, surveyed by N.G. Ranga, were making profits dealing in paddy[15]. The rich cultivators began investing in agro-industries, and built many new rice mills from the capital.

Ranga describes about the attempts by rich peasants in several Guntur villages to start business. "In every village, there were a few enterprising Kammas with 10 to 20 acres of land and were anxious to do some sort of business or other"[16]. Most of these ventures were unsuccessful, because of lack of sufficient capital and business capacity, business bent of mind and the lack of commercial organisation to advise people as well as prohibitive rates of interests. A new stratum of rich peasants emerged in the delta, developing into an entrepreneurial commercial farmer capitalist class, by early twentieth century.

**State Aid to Industries**

In the Madras Presidency, the State Aid to Industries Act was passed in 1923, which suggested that to promote the industry as recommended by the Indian Industrial Commission. The Government in the Northern Circars extended loans to industries, supplying commercial and industrial information, at concessional rates of transportation of raw material. The Government also started a few industries on experimental lines to serve as models to natives initiating industries on their own. It also opened several technical and industrial schools and provided scholarships to those students undergoing training at schools.

In the year 1931, Boddu Pydenna's Oil Mills of Vizianagaram were granted a loan of Rs. 50,000 for the purchase of oil expeller for crushing purpose and also for their standing capital[17]. In the year 1936, an amount of Rs. 40,000 was granted to Mr. Ramakrishna Ranga

Rao for their sugar mills at Kirlampudi, which enabled the industries to purchase new machinery. This addition of new machinery enabled them to raise their crushing capacity from 80 ton to 120 ton per day. A provision was also made for the purchase of shares,[18] but most of them did not fulfill the conditions required under the State Aid to Industries Act[19]. The Vuyyuru Cooperative Sugar Factory in Krishna district was granted a loan of Rs. 10,00,000 from the Madras Provincial Cooperative Bank. In the year 1925, the Rajahmundry Match Factory was granted free supplies of wood as raw material from the Government reserves[20]. The Rajahmundry Paper Industry was granted a protection in the form of supplies of bamboos from Rekapally reserves at concessional rates. The Government had laid down in their policy of industrial development of the provinces a provision for conducting experiments of few industries. The ultimate object was the starting of industries either by private owners, or by Government or new branches or improving the processes of existing industries.

In the year 1926, the department sanctioned Rs. 2,500 for experimenting on coir retting at Ambajipet. Similar help was reserved for such coir retting at Amalapuram also in the year 1937, which was continued in the year 1938 also. Similarly, experiments were conducted educating the natives in Circars about the improved methods of cane crushing using power centrifugals. Experiments were conducted at Munagapalla, Rayavaram, and the machinery was supplied to several entrepreneurs in several places free of lease.

## Promotion of Technical Education

The Government had granted funds for starting

industrial schools. St. Joseph Industrial School, Gunadala, Krishna district received grants for building purpose[21]. St. Alloysius Industrial School at Visakhapatnam received Rs.1,200 as grant-in-aid to take up instruction in Mathematics and Mechanical Engineering[22]. Other schools which received similar help were C.B.M Industrial School, Kakinada, Industrial School, Kowtavaram in Krishna District, Andhra Jateeya Vidyaparishad.[23] In these schools, the subjects like turner, smithy, woodworks, mechanical engineering, electrical works, paper making, motor works and agricultural studies were taught.

The development of sugar industry having created a demand for sugar technology, at Andhra University, B.Sc. (Hons) in the Chemical Technology, including Technology of Cane-Sugar, was taken up and the Government installed scholarships of value of Rs.40 each for students pursuing this course[24], from the year 1935.

## Modern Industries

The agro-industries such as jute, sugar, oil milling, tobacco, cashew nut roasting, and rice milling flourished in the Northern Circars during 1919-1939.

## Jute Mills

Four jute mills were located by the end of 1939 at Nalimerla, Chittivalasa, Eluru, and Guntur, in the entire presidency. The Krishna Jute and Cotton Mills Company Ltd., Eluru, carried on spinning and weaving. The company which was registered on the 18th July, 1904 in the office of Assistant Registrar of Joint Stock Companies, Machilipatnam, functioned as private limited concern with a authorised capital of Rs. 5,00,000 divided into 5,000 shares of Rs. 100 each. It was engaged in buying raw jute and manufacturing gunny bags, with a sum of Rs. 4,51,840 paid up till 1931. The mill started work in 1907 and the first dividend of Rs. 6 per share was declared in 1915. Upto 1928, a total of Rs.239 per share had been paid as dividend. The 1929 balance sheet showed a net loss of Rs. 14,010 for the year ending 31st December, 1930. The closure mill for 7 months and the fall of prices of gunny bags sustained the firm over a loss of Rs. 1,51,147[25]. The plant as on 1931 had 116 looms, 2530 spindles and all subsidiary machinery to it, 3 Lancashire boilers and Marshall's, compound horizontal engine of 750 HP with a mechanical shop with up-to-date machinery for repairs. There were 800 workers employed, for whom an amount of Rs. 6,64,200 p.a. was spent. It got a net profit of Rs. 24,000 p.a. The value of assets of the company as on 3rd March, 1931 was Rs. 7,35,719. The company paid income tax worth Rs. 3,77,689 on an average of Rs. 15,000 p.a.

**Oil Mills**

Vizianagaram, Godavari, and Guntur districts have had oil mills. Three oil mills at Vizianagaram found engaged in groundnut decorticating and oil milling, and the other two in ground nut decorticating and rice hulling. The three mills of Vizianagaram, Donkinavalasa and Komatipally were run by Boddu Pydanna Company of Vizianagaram. They have been running the mills since 1901. The mill was crushing kurinji, and vepa in the hand screw presses installed in their factory. The seeds were available in sufficient quantities. There was great demand for the vepa oil from Calcutta and Rangoon for soap making and for the kurinji from Cuttak, Eluru, Warangal and Bellary for tanning purposes. There were ten rotary mills whose capacity was 400 gallon or 3,600 Ibs of oil per diem of 11 hours. The value of the machinery, land buildings, in each factory costing Rs.61,752. About 20 persons were employed, and they were getting a profit of Rs.10,000 per year[26].

**Sugar Mills**

In the year 1933, on account of the protection extended, a great deal of public interest was concentrated for manufacturing of sugar in Madras Presidency. Some 20 factories each with 400 ton capacity per day expected to be set up in the Presidency.

There were a total of six sugar mills in the region during the period under study. They were Ramakrishna Sugar Mills Ltd. started by Kirlampudi Zamindar in the year 1935 and Samalkot Sugar Mill being the oldest floated by Parry and Co. Ltd. started in the first decade of the 20th century, the Etikopaka Sugar Mills at Etikopaka, the Visakhapatnam Sugar Mills. In the year 1934, the Raja of Bobbili started a sugar factory, the Sri Rama Sugar Industries Ltd. at Bobbili with a capital of 43.62 lakhs. In the year 1940, another sugar factory was floated in Srikakulam by the same Bobbili Raja with a capital of Rs.27.99 lakhs, which provided employment to 608 workers[27]. In the year 1933, a sugar factory was started at Thummapalla of Visakhapatnam and another in 1934 at Vuyyur of Krishna district[28].

**Tobacco Processing Units**

In Guntur district, tobacco cultivation took to commercial dimensions during 1919-39, with processing units. The Indian Leaf Tobacco Company Ltd. was installed for handling and redrying of tobacco at Chirala, and operated normally between 15 January and 1st August[29]. It is understood that in the year 1936, the tobacco growers and dealers in Guntur district had formed into a joint stock company with Rs. 6,00,000 capital divided into 60 thousand shares. The factory proposed to install the machinery necessary for curing and re-drying and storing purposes in Guntur[30].

## Conclusion

Madras government considered some seven applications out of 20 for loan under State Aid to Industries Act and granted a total sum of Rs. 2,00,000 during 1923-35. However, the Act failed to induce any confidence among people, though the results were unimpressive under financial terms. It was true that some of the initiatives meant a significant departure from earlier position.

During the inter-war years, the Northern Circars witnessed certain degree of dynamic change in economy and the development of industries along modern lines.

## References

1. Bipanchandra, *Rise and Growth of Economic Nationalism in India*, Delhi, 1996, p.113.
2. Suniti Kumar Ghosh, 'Indian Bourgeoisie and Imperialism', *Economic and Political Weekly*, Vol. XXIII, Nos. 45-46, Special number 1988, p. 2449.
3. *Ibid.*, p. 2450.
4. Indian Industrial Commission (1916-18) report, Delhi 1980, p. 286.
5. Dhiresh Bhattacharya, *A Concise History of the Indian Economy 1750-1950*, Progressive Publishers, Calcutta, 1972, p. 92.
6. *Annual Report of the Department of Industries for Year Ended with 31st March, 1921*, p. 2. Andhra Pradesh State Archives, Hyderabad.

7. K.S. Mathew, 'Masulipatnam and the Maritime Trade of India during the 17th Century', *Proceedings of A.P. History Congress*, Nagaram, 1987, p. 78.
8. *Ibid.*, 78.
9. *Ibid.*, 79.
10. G.N. Rao, 'Canal Irrigation and Agrarian Change in Colonial Andhra, A Study of Krishna District', *E.P.W.*, Vol. XX, Nos. 25 and 26, 1985, p. 60.
11. *Ibid.*, p. 60.
12. G.N. Rao, 'Canal Irrigation and Agrarian Change in Colonial Andhra, A Study of Godawari District', *E.S.H.R, .Vol. 25,* No. 1, p. 47.
13. Nata Duvvury, 'Tobacco Trading and Forms of Market Organisation', in K.N. Raj, (ed) *Essays on Commercialisation of Indian Agriculture*, Oxford University Press, USA, 1985, p. 234.
14. Carolyn Boyack Upadhyaya, 'The Farmer Capitalists of Coastal Andhra Pradesh', *E.P.W.*, Vol. 23, No. 27, 1988, July 2, p. 1377.
15. *Ibid.*, p. 1378.
16. *Ibid.*, p. 1380.
17. Government Order (hereafter G.O.) No. 1729. *Development Department*, Madras Government, dated 7th August, 1931, p. 8.
18. G.O. No. 1906, *Dev. Department*, Govt. of Madras, 3rd August, 1938.
19. *Annual Report of the Dept. of Industries, Govt. of Madras, for the Year Ending with 31st March, 1936.*
20. G.O. No.1163, *Dev. Dept.*, Govt. of Madras, dated 10th August, 1925.
21. Annual Rreport of the Dept. of Industries, for the Year Ending with 31st March, 1928.
22. *Ibid.*
23. *Ibid.*, year ending with 31st March, 1931.
24. *Ibid.*, year ending with 31st March, 1935.

25. G.O. No. 1273, *Dev. Dept.*, Govt. of Madras, dated 25th August, 1931.
26. G.O. No. 1179, *Dev. Dept.*, Govt. of Madras, dated 7th August, 1931.
27. AdibatlaVenkata Ramana, *Srikakulam Jilla Charitra* (telugu), Srikakulam, 1975, p. 312.
28. *Annual Report of Dept. of Industries, for the Year Ending with 31st March, 1935, Govt. of Madras.*
29. G.O.No. 1315, *Dev. Dept.*, Govt. of Madras, dated 27th October, 1933.
30. *Ibid.*

# 4

# Emergence of Landless Class in Colonial Southern India

*Devireddy Subramanyam Reddy*

Many new classes of people came into existence in southern India during the British colonial rule. These include: (1) the landed classes like *zamindari* proprietors (not owners) of land (both aristocratic as well as moneyocratic zamindars), the *pattadari* proprietors (not owners) of land, (like the *Ryotwari* peasants) and the non-cultivating/agriculturist landlords (coming from various professions, usurers or moneylenders and rich peasantry), (2) the landless classes like tenants (paying rent in money or kind or labour), the sharecroppers (sharers in crop with proprietors of land), the agricultural labourers ('free' or hired or seasonal labourers), the bonded labourers or serfs etc.; and also (3) the merchant bourgeois or middle class, (4) the industrial capitalists, (5) the finance capitalists, (6) the industrial working class, (7) the intelligentsia, etc.

As the subject of emergence of new classes in modern Indian society is a very vast one, the present paper confines only to the aspects of creation or emergence of landless class. This has special reference to the role of the British Ryotwari system of land revenue in southern India. The creation or contribution to the emergence of landless classes like (a) the tenants — paying rent in money, in kind and in labour (without remuneration), (b) the sub-tenants/ under-tenants, (c) the bargadars, (d) the sharecroppers and (e) the agricultural labourers (constituting seasonal labourers, hired labourers, also called 'free' labourers, and landlords labourers or agrestic serfs or simply serfs or bonded labourers/debt slaves) who could not provide any security of property for the loans required, was as a result of this.

The British East India Company secured Madras in 1639 and became an *inamdar*. It secured Sutanuti, Gobindpur and Calcutta in 1697 and became the first foreign and moneyocratic zamindar (not native and aristocratic zamindar). It secured 24-Parganas in 1757, secured the *Diwani* right over Bengal in 1765 and became far bigger zamindar. It established authority through war and diplomacy over the entire nation.

It introduced agrarian reforms in the form of Zamindari Permanent Settlements, and Ryotwari/ Pattadari Settlements, Mahalwari Settlements. Considering itself as the supreme landlord in India, it created a new class of landlords: (1) bigger proprietary landlords called Zamindars, (2) smaller proprietary landlords called Pattadari Ryots, and (3) village landlords called Mahalwari proprietors. The Company considered them as proprietors of land and not as the owners of land so long as they paid their *peshkash* (tribute) and 'rent' (land tax), respectively. The Company 'resumed' the land belonging to age-old original owners of land traditional ownership right, called occupancy right. One must note here that land belonged, originally, to the people who cleared bushes, cultivated crops, and paid tax. Once it happened, they became perpetual owners/occupants of that particular land ; even the king could not deny this traditional right. If the king or the queen wanted that land he or she had to buy that land by paying a price as we observed in the first land grant made to Tirumala Venkateswara by Samavai or Kadavan Perundevi in 966 AD.

After resuming the land belonging to the traditional owners/occupants, the Company Government vested the resumed land in the hands of the heads of villages, castes, religions, sects and other important people in the villages (under the Ryotwari System). The Company retained the remaining cultivable, waste and forest lands. The individuals in whose hands, the land was vested were not given ownership right over land; what they were given was only proprietary right over the land they received from the Company Government, thus transforming them into proprietors. And, this was done, even under Ryotwari, by way of direct agreements, resembling the system of capitalist contracts, between the Government and the proprietors with regard to the extent, quality, location, etc., of land taken and also the 'rent' to be paid by the proprietary Ryot. This kind of resumption of land from many and vesting the same in a few individuals resulted in the concentration of land in a few hands like *pattadars* and transformation of freely available land into saleable and, hence, valuable commodity and thus not easily acquirable by the rural folk. This situation naturally led to concentration of land in the hands of *pattadari* peasant proprietors under whom, of course, tenants, sub-tenants, under-tenants, came into existence in Ryotwari tracts and resulted in denial of land to millions of people. This, in turn, caused creation or emergence of a large body of landless classes like (1) tenants — (a) paying rent in money, (b) paying rent in kind or sharecroppers/*bargadars*, (c) paying rent in labour (unpaid labourers); (2) bonded labourers or serfs, and (3) agricultural labourers such as (a) seasonal labourers, (b) hired labourers and (c) 'free' labourers.

Similarly, the extraordinarily higher rate of 'rent' under Ryotwari system took away most of the income from the hands of the peasant proprietors and acted as a disincentive to agriculture. It further caused deterioration of agriculture and pauperised the so-called *pattadari* proprietary Ryots, thus contributing to the de-peasantisation process and emergence of landless class. This constituted of tenants, sub-tenants, sharecroppers, agricultural labourers, etc. Simultaneously, the lack of money led to lack of purchasing power, lack of food and starvation deaths, i.e., occurrence of artificial famines. For example, the rent collected in the Ryotwari ceded districts (present Rayalaseema of Andhra Pradesh excluding Chittoor, but including Bellary) was Rs. 12 lakh in 1800-01; it rose to Rs.1 7 lakh in 1801-02, Rs. 18 lakh in 1802-03, falling just to Rs. 17 lakh in the famine year of 1803-04, and again rising to Rs. 20.5 lakh in 1804-05, and to Rs. 23 lakh in 1805-06. Similarly, while the land tax per lakh of population was Rs. 10 lakh in Bengal, Rs. 17 lakh in Bombay, and Rs. 23 lakh in Madras. Madras Ryotwari tax thus remained the highest in the country. Particularly, the initial assessments made under Ryotwari were so excessive and the methods adopted to collect rent was so oppressive that the Government (especially at the insistence of Thomas Munro during his Governorship) had to reduce their demand of one-half of the estimated gross produce of the fields to one-third, which still proved to be considerably heavy. The oppressive situation worsened further on the demise of Munro. "For thirty years, the province of Madras became a scene of oppression and agricultural distress unparalleled even in India at that age." The situation led to such an uproarious debate in the British Parliament that the Government of India was forced to appoint a commission, popularly called the Torture Commission, to enquire into the whole affair, of course, in response to the submission of a report on the condition of the Ryotwari peasant by Gajula Lakshmi Narasu Chetty of the Madras Native Association in early 1850s. The results of investigation revealed the lands to have been oppressively assessed restarting torturous methods for the 'rent' collection. During Parliamentary enquiries of 1852-53, James William B. Dykes, a revenue official of Salem district deposed before the House of Commons about the evils of the then Ryotwari system such as: (1) the enhancement of assessment whenever cultivators improved their lands, (2) the uncertainty of tenure; and (3) the 'unintelligibility' of revenue rules to ignorant cultivators.

The abnormally higher rate of rent and the consequent low level of income to peasant proprietors (causing need of money), coupled with the right to sell, mortgage and transfer land (given under *Ryotwari patta* systems) increased the credit-worthiness of peasants, facilitating the rise of usurers or money-minded capitalist money lending class. The latter collected abnormal rates of interest, leading to indebtedness of peasantry over the transfer and concentration of land.

This was either (1) in the hands of cultivating/agriculturist landlord-cum-moneylender class (like the rich peasant of the later days) and other landlords, or (2) in the hands of the non-cultivating/agriculturist landlords like moneylenders, moneylending traders and other professionals, thrusting the growth of landless class. The British land revenue systems/policy as such increased the credit-worthiness of peasantry through proprietary title called *patta* to their land. The increased value of land (due to scarcity of land created by the British) made it a good security against loans. The moneylender was willing to give advances as legal machinery for enforcement of contract was well-established under British administration. All this led to unrestrained usury and chronic indebtedness in rural communities. As a result, land got transferred to non-cultivating/agriculturist moneylenders and caused growth of de-peasantisation process, and birth of landless class. Thus, there was close connection between Ryotwari and the debt problem.

On the other hand, the insistence of payments in money by the Government led to export of foodgrains to meet cash needs and raise commercial crops (commercialisation of agriculture). Export of foodgrains led to fall in food stocks, rise in price of foodgrains, rise in taxation to the extent of increase in income/revenue, fall in the buying capacity of peasants, and occurrence of artificial famines and further dependence on moneylenders for loans — for raising crops, for other agricultural needs or purchase of foodgrains (unproductive borrowing became necessary for household/domestic purposes due to insufficient income). Thus, commercialisation of agriculture could not ease financial burden of peasant as commercial crops could be raised by rich peasants and not by small peasants, who were large in number. The raising of commercial crops needed higher investment in agriculture, which the small peasants seldom could offer.

Under conditions of abnormally higher rate of rent, higher interest, lower income, unavoidable higher expenditure for agriculture, etc., deficient financing became a regular feature. In the absence of institutional financial support (from Government or banks or other financial institutions), it became necessary to depend for finance on moneylender of one kind or the other who acted as credit agency as well as marketing agency, and played the role of a double-edged sword in the rural economy. Hence, the peasant had no other alternative other than accepting, loan from moneylenders and live in debt their successors inheriting the burden. As Marx said, "Usury centralises money; it sucks out the peasants' blood." Thus, the sucking of peasants' blood by the state, on one hand, and the moneylender on the other demobilised peasants; even the extension of cultivation, increased production, commercialisation of agriculture, and increased revenue could not improve their condition This caused (1) increase in poverty, (2) sale, mortgage and transfer of land, and (3) fragmentation of landholdings into uneconomic size, ultimately throwing peasants into the web of indebtedness.

Though the credit/money needs of peasants were met from various sources, it was the moneylenders who provided (as per 1951 figures) about 70 per cent of the financial needs of peasants as:

| | | | *Per cent* |
|---|---|---|---|
| 1. | Moneylender | - | 28.3 |
| 2. | Landlords-cum-moneylenders | - | 39.9 |

| | | |
|---|---|---|
| 3. Village moneylender | - | 05.3 |
| 4. Tenants | - | 13.0 |
| 5. Government | - | 02.0 |
| 6. Banks | - | 05.3 |

Surprisingly, the main object of accepting loans was for food i.e., the growers of food (peasants) were securing food by raising loans. The rest was for interest payments and agricultural developments. This hindered growth of capitalist methods of production. The reasons for rise of moneylending class were thus: (1) higher rate of 'rent' or tribute, (2) monetisation of payments, (3) commercialisation of agriculture, (4) desperate attachment to land (5) lack of alternative sources of livelihood, and (6) lack of institutional credit.

Consequent on the higher rate of rent, moneylenders' abnormal rates of interest and commercialisation of agriculture, the indebtedness of peasant in India rose from Rs. 3,000 million in 1911 to Rs. 18,000 million in 1938, a six-fold increase. The indebtedness was so high that by 1951, the peasant was not in a position to engage agricultural labourers who constituted 35 per cent of the 71 per cent of the landless class by 1931. It may be noted that the landless class remain insignificant number before the British rule, but the bonded labourers — variously called as agrestic slaves, slaves, bonded labourers, serfs, debt slaves — who could not provide any security for loans from moneylenders, constituted just 2.7 per cent only; although a little higher in the European plantations. This percentage owed its existence to lack of alternative sources of livelihood and disintegration of bigger landholdings, which needed agrestic slaves. Moreover, the cost of maintenance of bonded labourers under petty mode of production was appreciably higher than the system of hiring 'free' labour.

It is interesting to note that the disintegration of peasantry was highest in southern India and next in eastern India. Similarly, the growth of agricultural labourers was the least or lower in northern India and western India respectively.

The average annual income of agricultural labourers was much less than the wages of industrial workers and other rural families at Rs. 32.7 and Rs.117.5, respectively. The standard of living of the former was much less compared with the latter. The reasons for this were: (1) obsolete methods of agricultural production on low profits and wages, (2) slow industrial development leading to unemployment and low income, (3) lack of labour organisation to protect their interest, (4) low level of agricultural production, and (5) the existence of caste or casteism.

The bonded labourers, were variously called as bonded labourers, bonded slaves, debt slaves, agrestic slaves, semi-serfs, serfs. It is interesting to note that bonded labourers did not increase much during colonial rule, in spite of pauperisation of tillers leading to indebtedness. In other words, bonded slavery was in check just 2.7 per cent of the landless agricultural labourers. The reasons for this were:

(1) the prevalence of commodity exchange and market relations which made maintenance of serf labour unproductive, (2) the existence of overpopulation and consequent availability of 'free' wage-labourers, (3) absence of large estates due to splitting of large estates or landholdings into small holdings, (4) petty mode of

production due to absence of large scale production, resulting from absence of large estates, and (5) existence of outmoded and backward technique of production.

The bonded labourers came into existence mainly during British rule. They were the poorest agricultural labourers. They came mostly from castes like Halis in Gujarat, Izhavas in Kerala, Pannial in Tamil Nadu, Kamyas in Bihar, etc.

The exorbitant rates of interest collected by moneylender-cum-land owners, and the inability of the debtors to provide any security of property forced them sign a pledge or agreement. As per pledge, the labourer becomes a slave of the debtor, losing freedom to work or serve for any land owner or master. His position becomes worse than the medieval serf. The modern bonded-labourer was provided neither land nor full employment by the master or by the medieval master.

This debt slavery gave stability to caste system. The south and north-east Indian labourers were the worst victims of this debt slavery. Although, the British Government rectified several laws to eradicate slavery in 1843, 1859, 1923, 1926, 1929, it empowered Europeans owning plantations, hiring bonded-labourers or slaves in plantations, more particularly in the north-eastern India, where 'free' wage-labourers were not available. It is interesting to note that a large number of these bonded-labourers working in the north-eastern plantations were from southern India; southern plantations engaged mostly 'free' labourers, since they were available in large number.

It is also necessary to note that the *inam/miras* or permanent private property right in land (just as in kind or in office) given for the services rendered to the society or the state was also resumed, under Ryotwari, and brought under regular and heavy taxation or 'rent' as, for example, in the ten Chittoor Palems, the Sarkar territories, the Koilkuntla Palem of Majjara Narasimha Reddy in the present Rayalaseema region of Andhra Pradesh. This had, in fact, resulted in the rebellion of Chittoor Palegars during 1801-05, the no-tax movement of Ryotwari peasants of Chittoor during the same period and the uprising of Koilkunta Narasimha Reddy in 1846.

We may note here that by October 30, 1869 there were 452 categories of *inam* or privileged landholdings in Madras Presidency. These could be grouped under four heads, namely, (1) Socio-religious holdings or *devadayams*, (2) Socio-political holdings, (3) Social service holdings or *dharmadayams*, and (4) Socio-economic holdings. The first category of inams gifted to institutions and individuals include *inams* for temples, *muths*, and *matthams* and of the *lingayats*, *jangams*, *pandarams*, *bairagies*, or *varagis*, *waqfs* and *muafies*, masjids or mosques, *takiyas* or "pillows", *fakirs*, *dargahs*, *agraharams*, *brahmanadayams*, *shotriyams*, *bhattaviritties*, *khairaties*, etc. The second category include the *dorasthanams*, *bissois*, *samsthanams*, *mukhasas* and *gramamanyams*. The third category include *inams* for maintenance of *chattrams/charadies/choultries*, *nirrlu-pandals*, *topes*, *nandanavanams*, wells, ponds, tanks, canals, *patasalas*, *langarkhanas*, etc. The last category include the *dasbandams* and *maramat inams*. The *inams* had gradually become symbols of accumulated status, power, privilege, influence, charity and the subsistence of entrenched privilege and power for every important institution or elite group of the country. The tampering or interference with *inam* as a result, during the British period led to discontent and rebellion against the British in innumerable places like Chittoor, Koilkuntla, etc.

In the case of village communities, different sections or communities, as noted earlier, held hereditary privileges in land, grain, office, etc., as hereditary property/right or *mirasi/inam* in land, grain, office, etc. It is also interesting to note that every one in the village, whether office holder or non-office holder, or peasant or non-peasant, held land on some tenure or the other and with tax exemption or concession or on full payment and, at the same time, pursued his traditional and hereditary profession. In case of heavy taxation, they became landless or migrated to places, where taxation was low. The denial (to the village community/panchayat) of the right to distribute and redistribute land periodically among peasants establishing economic equality among villager's yielded to landlessness besides unemployment in place of self-sufficiency among the village communities.

A rough percentage of different categories of agricultural labourers in colonial India as in 1931 was described under.

From the table below, it is clear that 71 per cent were without landed rights (total of IIb, IIb and IV). About 35 per cent out of 71 per cent were agricultural labourers, either full-time employed or under-employed. Of this, 2.7 per cent out of 71 per cent were bonded labouerers, with dominance of wage-labourers. About 1/3rd of agricultural working population were small land holding labourers.

Like the peasant community, the artisans were ruined during the British rule and many of them became

**Agricultural Population - Categories**

| | *Social Composition in 1931* | *Number in millions in 1931* | *Percentage in 1931* | |
|---|---|---|---|---|
| (I) | Total agricultural population | 111 | 100.0 | |
| | (a) Rent receivers | 4 | 003.6 | Land |
| (II) | Farmers cultivating more than five acres | 28 | 025.3 | |
| | (a) Owner cultivators | 18 | 016.3 | Land |
| | (b) Tenants | 10 | 009.0 | L.T (1) |
| (III) | Dwarf holding labourers | 37 | 033.3 | |
| | (a) Petty proprietors | 10 | 009.0 | Landed |
| | (b) Tenants at will and share-croppers | 27 | 024.3 | L.T (2) |
| (IV) | Landless agricultural labourers | 42 | 037.8 | L.T. (3) |
| | (a) Bonded labourers | 03 | 002.7 | |
| | (b) Unemployed labourers | 35 | 031.5 | |
| | (c) Full-time free wage-labourers | 04 | 003.6 | |

landless, forced to work in the company's 'factories'. They were not allowed to leave the factory, until the entrusted work or allowed to work for other companies or individuals. They were forced to accept advances and produce goods for the company and remain forever bonded/debt slaves of the Company. They were paid meagre remuneration, forced to sell goods at one-fourth of face value; sometimes even seized without payment. Their products were made to become monopoly of the Company since the British rule of 1757 till the introduction of *laissez-fair* or free trade policy in 1813. Subsequently, the manufactures of England were allowed under free trade to flood Indian markets. This led to unequal competition between products of England and handicrafts or those of India and consequent destruction of native industry as well as of the age-old "union between agriculture and manufacturing industry", which was promoting inter-dependence or balanced development of industry and agriculture. This, in turn, crippled the centuries-old world famous native industry and contributed to the process of deindustrialisation, gradual ruinisation of artisan communities (or native industry), destruction of native knowhow, and the consequent shift of several artisans to agricultural sector as tenants or sharecroppers or agricultural labourers — overburdening agriculture, fall in per capita income and buying or spending capacity of people which, in turn, increased the frequency of artificial famines and starvation deaths, a sign of increasing ruralisation.

Similarly, the Indian merchant communities seldom bought goods directly from producers since the Company maintained monopoly in Indian trade between 1757-1813. They had to buy goods only from the Company, at a higher price, resulting in lower profits. They were forced to become either (1) the underlings of the Company or its servants engaged in private trade or private British merchants, or (2) give up traditional trading profession, or (3) become petty intermediaries between the British and the native producers, or (4) shift to agricultural sector as farmers of revenue or as landless class of tenants or sharecroppers or agricultural labourers and live in poverty. On the other hand, the heavy taxation on world famous Indian handmade goods exported to England, and the little or no taxation on the British machine-made goods imported into India resulted in the decline of export at the cost of increased import (in the unequal trade under the so-called free trade policy of 1813), thereby reducing trading opportunities to natives. Efforts were made to increase the raw material export, particularly commercial (agricultural) produces needed for British industry in England.

The discriminatory policies in tariff and customs duties, in tax on sale, and in goods transport rates in railways ruined the native trading communities. This resulted in the shift of several native traders or businessmen to agriculture sector as tenants or sharecroppers or agricultural labourers, resulting in overburden on agriculture, fall in per capita income and buying capacity, growth of artificial famines and starvation deaths. This mode of ruinisation of trading communities, in turn, delayed the emergence of an independent native merchant bourgeois or middle class and growth of capitalist economy for a long period. The drain or pumping out of Indian capital and wealth to England starved India of the capital and prevented accumulation of capital in the hands of natives. As

Edmund Burke said, "Every rupee of profit made by an Englishman is lost forever to India."

The inevitable changes ultimately led to the disappearance of land and profession from the hands the peasants, artisans and business and trading communities.

## References


- T.H. Beaglehole, *Thomas Munro and the Development of Administration Policy in Madras (1792-1818): The Origins of Munro System*, London, 1816.
- G.R. Gelig, *Life of Sir Thomas, Munro,* 3 Vols., London, 1830.
- J.A. Arbuthnot, *Sir Thomas Munro: Selections from his Minutes and other Official Writings,* 2 Vols., London, 1888.
- *The Fifth Report (edited by Walter Kelly Firminger) of the Select Committee of the House of Commons on the Affairs of The East India Company,* Madras, 28th July 1812, Calcutta, Vol. II.
- N. Anjaniah and S.V. Bhende, *Studies in the Taxation of Agricultural Land and Income in India,* 1965.
- Nilamani Mukherjee, 'The Ryotwari System and Mirasi Rights in Madras Presidency,' in the *Indian History Congress Proceedings of the Twenty Third Session* held at Aligarh in 1961, Part II, Calcutta, 1961.
- Nilamani Mukherjee, *Ryotwari System in Madras, 1792-1827,* Firma, Calcutta, 1962.
- Robert Eric Frykenberg (ed), *Land Control and Social Structure in Indian History,* Madison, 1969 ; 'Company Circari in the Carnatic, c. 1799-1859 : The Inner Logic of Political System in India,' in Richard G. Fox (ed), *The Realm and Region in Traditional India,* New Delhi, 1977, 'The Silent Settlement in Southern India, 1793-1853: An Analysis of the Role of the Indian Imperial System,' in Robert

Frykenberg (ed), *Land Tenure and Peasant in Southern Asia,* New Delhi, 1977.

- B.H. Baden-Powell, *The Land Systems of British India,* Vol. III, Oxford, 1892, reprint, Delhi, 1974; *A Short Account of the Land Revenue and its Administration,* Oxford, 1913.
- Burton Stein, *Thomas Munro,* Oxford University Press, New Delhi, 1989.
- *The Humble Petition of the Madras Native Association and Others, Native Inhabitants of the Presidency of Madras, dated 10th December 1852,* Madras, in appendix to the Report from the Select Committee on Indian Territories, 1852, in India Office Library, London.
- *Report of the Commission for Investigation of Alleged Torture in Madras Presidency,* Madras, 1855, in printed sources in Tamil Nadu Archives, Madras, Vol. ASO (D) 432.
- *Inam Commission Report* by W.T. Blair (Officiating Inam Commissioner) to R.A. Dalyell (Acting Secretary to Government, Revenue Department, Fort St. George), dated October 30, 1869, Madras.
- M.P.R. Reddy (Malli Reddy Pattabhi Rama Reddy), *Peasant and State in Modern Andhra History,* Clio Club, Kavali, 1986; *Gajula Lakshmi Narasu Chetty: Life and Times (1806-1868),* Kavali, 1985.
- Bhovani Sen, *Evolution of Agrarian Relations in India,* Peoples Publishing House, New Delhi, 1962.
- Sunil Sen, *Agrarian Relations in India, 1793-1947,* New Delhi, 1979.
- Romesh Chunder Dutt, *The Economic History of India under Early British Rule,* Routledge and Kegan Paul Ltd., London, 1950.
- R. Palme Dutt, *India Today,* Peoples Publishing House Ltd., Bombay, 1949.
- A.V. Ramana Rao, *The Economic Development of Andhra Pradesh, 1766-1957,* Bombay, 1958.

– Walter C. Neale, *Economic Change in Rural India,* Yale University Press, New Haven, 1962.

– R. Mukherjee, *Economic History of India, 1600-1880,* Longmans Green and Co., London, 1939.

– V.B. Singh, *Economic History of India, 1857-1956,* Allied Publishers Pvt. Ltd., New Delhi, 1975.

– *Selection of Papers Relating to the Revolt of the Poligar Narasimha Reddy of Koilkuntla,* in 5 Vols., in Tamil Nadu State Archives, Madras, in printed original sources, Vols. ASO (D) (83-87) 111-115.

– D. Subramanyam Reddy, *Anti-British Revolts in Andhra with Special Reference to the Palegars of Chittoor Pollams, 1801-1805,* Ph.D thesis, Sri Venkateswara University, Tirupati, 1988.

# 5

# Capitalism, Colonial State and Indentured Labour from India

*G. Chandhrika*

## Introduction

*No gold did they find*

*Underneath any stone they*

*Touched and turned*

*Yet*

*Every stone they touched*

*Into solid gold they turned.*[1]

The rise and consolidation of global capitalism in post-enlightenment Europe is concommitant with the constitution of a labour subject, an autonomous and free individual, participating in a market governed by the economic laws of supply and demand, a product of the universal category of capitalism. Even as Marx claimed that it was "the universalising tendency of capital, which distinguishes it from all previous stages of production," he observed that the capital's tendency towards universality "will drive towards its own suspension."[2] The inner contradictions of capitalism are demonstrated in the apparent coexistence of free wage labour and unfree labour in the age of imperialism as in the case of indentured labour from India to different parts of British Empire. In free labour, economic compulsion plays a major role in exploiting and retaining labour power through the mediating institution of labour market wherein buyers and sellers have the freedom to return at will. In contrast, unfree labour refers to labour power governed by politico-legal mechanism and physical compulsion characterised by the absence of labour market or circumstances where the former limit the exchange of labour power within such labour market.[3]

The production of tropical commodities and precious metals sustained European trading empires on coerced labour sustaining production. The triangular flow of capital, commodities and labour primarily between Europe, Africa, and the Americas was the precursor of modern global capitalism. Capitalism in the age of imperialism set in motion a search for legal framework that could legitimise the dispossession of rights of the colonised people. Already, the history of England bore witness to the coercive law in the form of Enclosure Acts and Game Laws in the process of dispossessing rural farmers, hunters, and other subsistence producers, turning them into migrant labourers in search of livelihood in the free-wage market. The present work analyses the role of colonial state to control labour through legislation and the establishment of the indenture system of labour in the British Empire in the nineteenth century in the context of the global expansion of capitalism.

British rule in India was sustained not merely by military conquest, but more importantly by ideologies of dominance. Bernard S. Cohn in his influential work, *Colonialism and its Forms of Knowledge*, points how the British in India "invaded and conquered not only territory but an epistemological space as well."[4] The legitimisation of theory and practice of British rule necessitated the constitution of discursive space, namely, that of a "traditional Indian society". This unchanging and backward Indian society provided the conceptual framework for intellectual theorisation and the liberal-imperial agenda of modernisation. The introduction of English education and Anglo-Indian law proved to be two major domains, which witnessed the direct intervention of colonial state in the everyday life of the colonised. They provided the ideological apparatuses for the British to create and control the colonial "subject". If English education was a non-coercive strategy of control, Anglo-Indian law was a coercive strategy that reconstituted Indian subjectivity to suit British interests.[5] The centrality of law in the colonising process, especially in the case of India, has already received attention.[6] The early example of the Anglo-Indian law which touched upon labour was the Indian Penal Code, enacted by the British Parliament in 1860.

**Macaulay's Penal Code**

The Indian Penal Code, the first of its kind to be adopted in the British Empire, was crafted in 1837 by

Thomas Macaulay, Member of the Governor General's Legislative Council (1834-38). A lawyer-turned-reformist-politician, Macaulay was a contributor to the Reforms Act of 1832, the India Charter Act of 1833 and the Imperial Abolition of Slavery (1833-34) before his arrival in India. He was influenced by Jeremy Bentham's utilitarian ideas of scientific jurisprudence and the post-Napoleonic Europe's engagement with systematic codification of law. An abolitionist father and his associates, William Wilberforce and James Stephen, had also influenced him to the effect that the rule of law was the ground for England's moral conquest of India. He wrote to his father from India:

> *In a few months, I hope in a few weeks, we shall send up the Penal Code to Government. We have got rid of the punishment of death, except in the case of aggravated treason and willful murder. We shall also get rid indirectly of everything that can properly be called slavery in India. There will remain civil claims on particular people for particular services, which claims may be enforced by civil action; but no person will be entitled, on the plea of being the master of another, to do anything to that other which it would be an offence to do to a free man.*[7]

The IPC had five sections dealing with slavery and the sale of persons. The provisions did not make existing slavery an offence or abolish its practice but punished any transaction in slaves. In addition to assaults and similar physical offences against the body, for which masters were fully liable, the provisions most pertinent to labour exploitation were wrongful restraint, confinement, abduction, sale and kidnapping.

An attempt to make the law, and by extension British colonial rule, more effective and legitimate, the IPC was also crafted within a broader context of the contentious shift from slavery to indentured labour in the planter colonies.[8] The Indian Penal Code included some retrograde changes after Macaulay drafted it and despite punitive provisions it neither ended slavery in India nor put off the new indentured system of labour exploitation. The economic imperatives and political ends of imperialism proved rather strong for mild liberal impulses. The Indian Penal Code, a failed attempt of Benthamite utilitarianism, is a standing evidence of the limits of colonial legal reform. It marked the shift from slavery to indentured labour, integrating India onto the world system. It involved the shift in the source of labour from Africa to Asia. The abolition of slavery was followed by rapid growth of an imperial system of indenture, resulting in the recruitment and transportation of labourers from India.

**"Gladstone's Coolies"**

Indenture is defined as "an economically-induced migration, combined with coercive contractual obligations."[9] Indentured labour was first introduced in the tea plantations in colonial India.[10] The commercialisation of agriculture, destruction of traditional industries, cash demand for rent and other coercive measures, set in motion by colonial state, forced the population to face duress in the form of relocation of local economy, forcible evictions from land, unemployment and a massive disruption of livelihood. Famine and scarcity, which occurred with increasing frequency during the 1860s and 1870s in India, led to a general atmosphere of low morale. Peasants were forced to mortgage lands; the landless labourers were worst hit. Poverty and rural indebtedness made them destitute. The indentured labour system seemed to offer them a way out of the distress. The migrant labourers indentured themselves abroad, driven by privation, on the one hand, and lured by promises of opportunities elsewhere, on the other. Munshi Rahman Khan's *Jeevan Prakash*, the only available personal narrative of an indentured labourer in Surinam, shares about the recruiters' tales of greener pastures in plantations abroad.[11] Mabel Palmer, writing *The History of Indians in Natal*, observed:

> (T)he coming of the Indians to Natal was no spontaneous uncontrolled movement of adventurous individuals seeking a better livelihood than their home country gave them. It was part of an elaborate system organised and controlled by the governments of Great Britain and India.[12]

John Gladstone, a Liverpool merchant, Member of Parliament and father of British Prime Minister, William Ewart Gladstone, was the first planter ever to exploit indentured labour from India in his sugar plantations in Jamaica and Demerara, British Guiana, after the abolition of slavery.[13] Having learnt that Gillanders and Arbuthnot, a Calcutta-based firm, had sent Indian labourers to Mauritius, at half labour of a slave,[14] he solicited a similar service for his West Indian plantations in 1836. The effort bore fruit and the first set of some 396 indentured labourers from India, popularly called "Gladstone's coolies", arrived in British Guiana from Calcutta.[15] Indentured labour from India soon replaced slave labour in the sugar plantations of British West Indies. India became the main source of labour to planter colonies of European colonial empire. According to David Northrup, about 1.3 million Indians migrated between 1831 and 1920 to British Guiana, Trinidad, Jamaica, Mauritius, Reunion, French Caribbean, Dutch Guiana, East Africa, Natal and Fiji.[16]

Robert Miles identifies indenture system as one of the unfree labour system from capitalism and coexistence of different modes of production. He discusses two forms of indentured labour; one that was utilised in the Caribbean in the seventeenth and eighteenth centuries and another in the nineteenth century in the British Empire following the abolition of slave labour. He points out how in the case of the latter the "state served more directly as a contract enforcement agency, reinforcing the relations of direct domination of the non-producer over the producer." In the nineteenth century, the state played a crucial role in the establishment of the indentured labour and the accompanying migration.[17]

## The Role of Colonial State

Abolition of Britain's slave trade in 1807 and slavery in 1834 brought unprecedented change. The colonial administration provided a system of labour migration through which more than a million Indians signed contracts of indenture and migrated to Mauritius, British Guiana, Surinam, South Africa, the Caribbean islands, and Fiji. The recruitment and transportation of such labour were not regulated by any law when the colonial government of India, under the imperical Act V of 1837, laid down specific conditions, endorsing administrative framework to govern indenture system.[18] This legislation brought indentured labour under the colonial government's supervision. The colonial government succeeded in institutionalising the system of indentured labour, in favour of planters. Had the colonial government laid down the conditions of indenture, the planters were the ones who held control over the repressive apparatus, such as the courts, police, and prisons, which repressed workers. The contractual engagement was civil, where the breach of conditions by workers turned out to have penal consequences. The rights and duties embodied in the regulations were neither negotiated nor negotiable by the indentured labourers. A labourer was tied by the terms of engagement to particular employer and a particular residence. It was not legally possible for the migrant to change job or move freely outside the estate of his employer. The planters deployed formal and informal systems of control to confine workers. Indentured labour was underpinned by an elaborate system of coercion unlike free labour, driven by market rationality. The coercive aspects of the recruitment and shipment of indentured labourers, working practices on plantations, and the everyday and extraordinary lives of these migrant men and women have been brought out meticulously by a generation of economic and social historians.[19] It is possible to paint a general picture of plantation life that remains unchanged from the days of slavery. Imperialism provided the context for transition from slavery to indenture and the colonial legal apparatus succeeded in creating a "labour subject" that replaced the "slave" in the ideological discourse of British Imperialism.

## References

1. Mauritian poet, Vishwamitra Ganga Ashutosh, cited in the Report on the High Level Committee on the Indian Diaspora,

vi, http://indiandiaspora.nic.in/diasporapdf/part1-for.pdf, accessed on 7th April, 2013.

2. Karl Marx, *Grundrisse,* Harmondsworth: Penguin, 1973, 408 -410.
3. Robert Miles, *Capitalism and Unfree Labour: Anomaly or Necessity?* (London: Taylor and Francis, 1987) 171.
4. Bernard S. Cohn, *Colonialism and its Forms of Knowledge: The British in India,* New Delhi: Oxford UP, 1997, 4.
5. Valerian DeSousa, 'Strategies of Control: The Case of British India', *Sociological Viewpoints* (Fall, 2008) 61 – 74.
6. See Radhika Sinha, *A Despotism of Law: Crime and Justice in Early Colonial India*, Delhi: Oxford UP, 1998; Karuna Mantena, *Alibis of Empire: Henry Maine and the Ends of Liberal Imperialism*, Priceton: Princeton UP, 2010.
7. Thomas Macaulay to Zachary Macaulay, Calcutta, 12 October 1836, cited in Barry Wright, "Macaulay's Indian Penal Code and Codification in the Nineteenth Century British Empire" *Journal of Commanwealth Criminal Law* (May, 2012) 25.
8. Barry Wright, 25- 50.
9. Marina Carter, "Strategies of labour mobilisation in Colonial India: The Recruitment of Indentured Workers for Mauritius" in E. Valentine Daniel, Henry Bernstein, Tom Brass (Ed.), *Plantations, Peasants and Proletariat in Colonial Asia* (London: Routledge,1992) 229.
10. See Ranajit Das Gupta, "From Peasants and Tribesmen to Plantation Workers: Colonial Capitalism, Reproduction of Labor Power and Proletarianisation in North East India, 1850s to 1947", *Economic and Political Weekly*, 21 . 4 (Review of Political Economy, Jan. 1986) 2-10.
11. Kathinka Sinha- Kerkhoff, Ellen Bal and Alok Deo Singh Translators, *Autobiography of an Indian Indentured Labourer: Munshi Rahman Khan (1874 – 1972)* (Delhi, Sipra Publications, 2005) 71-76.
12. Mabel Palmer, *The History of Indians in Natal,* (London: University Press, 1957) 18.

13. For full details see Madhavi Kale, *Fragments of Empire: Capital, Slavery, and Indian Indentured Labor Migration in the British Caribbean* (Philadelphia: University of Pennsylvania Press, 1998) 13-37.
14. S.G. Checkland, *The Gladstones: A Family Biography 1764-1851*, (London, Cambridge UP, 1971) 318.
15. Basdeo Mangru, "Indian Labour in British Guiana", *History Today*, Volume: 36 Issue: 4 1986.
16. David Northrup, *Indentured Labour in the Age of Imperialism, 1834-1922* (Cambridge: Cambridge University Press, 1995), 156.
17. Robert Miles, 175.
18. Hugh Tinker, *A New System of Slavery: The Export of Indian Labour Overseas 1830-1920,* (Oxford: Oxford UP, 1974), 64.
19. See for example Richard B. Allen, *Slaves, Freedmen and Indentured Laborers in Colonial Mauritius* (Cambridge: Cambridge University Press, 1999); Marina Carter, *Servants, Sirdars and Settlers: Indians in Mauritius, 1834-1874* (New Delhi: Oxford University Press, 1995); Marina Carter, *Voices from Indenture: experiences of Indian migrants in the British Empire* (London: Leicester University Press, 1996); David Dabydeen and Brinsley Samaroo (eds), *India in the Caribbean* (London: Hansib, 1987); Kay Saunders (ed.), *Indentured Labour in the British Empire 1834-1920* (London: Croom Helm, 1984); Verene A. Shepherd, *Maharani's Misery: narratives of a passage from India to the Caribbean* (Mona, Jamaica: University of West Indies Press, 2002); Hugh Tinker, *A New System of Slavery: The Export of Indian labour Overseas 1830-1920* (Oxford: Oxford University Press, 1974).

# 6

# Colonial State in India : A Critical Appraisal

*K. Venugopal Reddy*

Colonisation works to decivilise the coloniser, to brutalise him in the true sense of the word, to degrade him, to awaken him to buried instincts, to covetousness, violence, race hatred and moral relativism.[1]

*Aimé Césaire*

The West won the world not by the superiority of its ideas or values or religion (to which few members of other civilisations were converted) but rather by its superiority in applying organised violence. Westerners often forget this fact, non-Westerners never do.[2]

*Samuel P. Huntington*

The statements aptly encapsulate the ruthless process of India's colonisation by the British and also "of spaces blanked out by that ruthless whiteness"[3] in the second half of the eighteenth and first half of the nineteenth centuries.

A

**Introduction**

Colonialism, perceived as a system of administration functioned primarily for the advantage of the coloniser. It ensured the perpetual and prolonged exploitation of the colonised people. It dislocated indigenous cultures and reoriented the patterns of progress in different segments of colonised space, throttling the manifestation of innovation. Colonisation has overwhelmingly fashioned the contours of institutional development around the world.[4] It consolidated the hegemony of coloniser over the colonised world. India was not an exception to such development. So, the distinctive feature of colonialism was its 'alienness',[5] the existence and the role of colonial state were to reinforce and advance such 'alienness'.[6] It was this 'alienness' and the process of colonising and subordinating indigenous people, that characterise the nature of such colonial state. Hence, it played a critical role in the trajectory of under development and uneven growth in diverse sectors of India.

India was known for its extensive trade in cotton textiles, which were in demand elsewhere in the world, particularly Africa, Europe, and West Asia. It is noted that '...India had a massive balance of trade surplus with Europe and West Asia, based mostly on its more efficient low cost cotton textile production and also of course on pepper for export. These went westwards to Africa, West Asia, Europe, and from thereon across the Atlantic to the Caribbean and the Americas.'[7] India had thus witnessed a robust and "...continued economic expansion...through the 17th century." However, the conquest of India and the establishment of British colonial rule in the second half of 18th century and the consolidation of colonial rule by mid-19th century had irretrievably altered the basic nature of its political, economic and social landscape.[9] India thus became a prey to British coloniser's relentless economic quest,[10] leaving it at last extremely emaciated in 1947.

**B**

**India in the Imagination of British Coloniser**

The British colonial rule in India had been justified by its conquest.[11] The idea that the British as a coloniser had an unassailable right to govern the colonised space was perceptible from the initial phase of their colonisation. Therefore, British colonialism, ever since its establishment in the mid-eighteenth century, primarily served the interests of the coloniser. It formidably strengthened and promoted the hegemony of the coloniser over the colonised people,[12] disturbing the indigenous cultures and reorienting the patterns of progress. It effectively constrained any manifestation of resistance in those territories. In the process, it ensured the unremitting and protracted exploitation of the colonised people.[13]

The British dominance established around the mid-18th century got entrenched in all spheres of India.[14] It was amply demonstrated in the representation of Indian people and their history.[15] The alien dominance got deeply embedded in the "distorted representation" of India denying it the "voice, autonomy, and agency".[16] Its materialisation was marked in "...objectification and re-ordering through the application of European scholarly methods on Indian thought and culture..."[17] Colonial power was demonstrated not just through the spread of its 'English ideas here and there, but upon the systematic redefinition and transformation of the terrain on which the life of the colonised was lived.'[18] The perception of India and its history, attitudes, morals, culture and customs was thus coloured by the prejudices of the colonisers. Significantly,[19] they presented their perception of history of India.[20] It should be read in that mode only. To argue that they presented an objective account of the history is only to think the colonisers way.[21]

The colonial dominance was firmly buttressed through 'baring the differences, real or assumed, and stamping its supremacy.'[22] It subsisted on continued perpetuation of violence and brutality, which were used as essential means for maintaining its control over the colonised. The colonial regime was always conscious of maintaining its image of power as something "unshakable in its expansive dominance". In India, as elsewhere, "deference and distance" were considered necessary for white dominance.[23]

Colonialism was not just a lived experience of the colonised, but also of the colonisers.[24] However, the colonisers constructed the colonised as the 'Other' and dealt with them as though they were inferior. The colonisers habitually disregarded the colonised in importance, endeavouring to cast natives in a very depreciatory mould. They constructed the native space dismally and characterised its people in a disparaging fashion against peace and progress. They justified their expansionist design through discourse on native people and their history with judgmental and condemnatory depictions.[25]

In Madras, the colonial administrators found the country "in a most unsettled state" and in the hands of "turbulent chieftains". The Polygars, who were ruling in the ceded districts in Andhra numbering about eighty and commanding 30,000 armed persons,[26] were represented to be "a nest of robbers" and the peasants and the country were portrayed to be "tormented by a continual state of violence and rapine." It was claimed that such an "unsettled country was ceded to the British." The British government was confronted with the problem of bringing "order and good government" to such a country, which witnessed "anarchy and robbery".[27] The colonisers normalised India by mid-nineteenth Century, defining its space as "an unchanging text" of primitive and static Hinduism—which reaffirmed the colonial regime as necessary moral and civilising order.[28] The introduction of land tenure systems in Bengal and Madras after 1793 and the subsequent spring of anti-British resistance movements in India were the outcome.[29]

**Dominance and Resistance**

Contemporary social theory is awash with hermeneutics of key concepts of 'Dominance' and 'Resistance'.[30] The two key concepts refer to 'complex of interconnections and relations' that constitute the society. In this sense, dominance and resistance are the two key concepts, with which the nature of social relations is to be grasped. They do signify the multiple layers of internal as well as external social reality. Theoretical interventions by historians, namely the Subalterns, have not adequately addressed the two concepts and it is forcibly argued that "Certainly, there is no concerted attempt to construct a theory of domination as hegemony, as the invocation of Gramsci might have led us to expect...The concepts of power which have actually been developed in the series are fragmentary and somewhat disconnected."[31] Similarly, on the aspect of the subalterns resistance to the domination of the colonial State or the 'elites' sections, these historians have failed to offer a convincing "theory of popular consciousness and resistance."[32]

The phenomenon of colonialism and the experience undergone by the colonised during the process of colonisation was not dissimilar globally and the colonial regimes are universally known for "marginalisation of resistance".[33] And yet the resistance of the colonised against the multiple forms of oppression by the colonisers was articulated through diverse ways. The process of colonisation in Asia, Africa or even Latin American countries met with a very stiff resistance from the indigenous communities, essentially from those sections that were mostly affected by this process.[34] Therefore, an attempt is made to present the trajectory of this colonial dominance and the resistance engendered in colonial India.

'The geographies of dominance and resistance are treated in a dynamic and networked way.'[35] It is argued that the 'spatialities of domination' and 'geographies of resistance' are constitutive of the domain of the relations of power, and they are not separated by the spatiotemporal activity. It is explained that resistance is incessantly intertwined with the relations of power and domination since "resistance turns up in domination" and 'domination turns up in resistance'.[36] On the manifestation of colonial power and its diverse forms of domination, Rosalind O' Hanlon explains thus "...it imposes a total milieu, institutions as well as intellectual and informational, to whose hegemonic sway its subjects must inevitably succumb. Colonial power thus derives its strength from two sources: from the material ability to coerce, which it brings with it in its armies, and from the Orientalist discourses of its second, shadow army of textual scholars, linguists, historians, anthropologists and so on."[37]

Just as there are myriad forms of dominance, there are also numerous modes of resistance against the structures of dominance. What constitutes resistance and who names it are challenging questions, which perhaps provoke equally challenging responses from those who dominate and those who offer resistance on "everyday" basis. Their perceptions can be diametrically apart. The scholars who 'developed this concept of resistance argued that opposition to domination takes myriad forms'.[38] Similarly, the responses to such 'opposition to domination' can also take myriad forms. Many scholars have focused on the term resistance, explaining "a wide variety of actions and behaviours at all levels of human social life (individual, collective, and institutional) and in a number of different settings, including political systems, entertainment and literature and workplace. Indeed, everything from revolutions to hairstyles has been described as resistance. The term is defined variously as, for example, "acting autonomously, in [one's] own interests"; "active efforts to oppose, fight, and refuse to cooperate with or submit to ... abusive behaviour and control"; "engaging in behaviours despite opposition"; or simply "questioning and objecting".[39]

The scholars explained that the word 'resistance' implies 'two elements' which 'were common to nearly explanations of the term'. The first is 'a sense of action' and the second involves 'a sense of opposition.' Hence, the core elements which 'resistance' embodies are 'action and opposition.'[40] The resistance can be expressed through open and massive protest movements or revolutions. It can also be articulated through "everyday" forms, which are 'prosaic and constant struggle.' These forms of resistance constitute 'the ordinary weapons of relatively powerless groups: foot dragging, dissimulation, false compliance, pilfering, feigned ignorance, slander, arson, sabotage, and so forth.'[41] These acts of 'everyday' forms of resistance may not make "headlines", but surely and quietly leave their footprints on the oppressive system.[42] Resistance or protest movements are not "...mechanically determined by social structure." It may be stated that the "defiance" could be "contingent on historical circumstance".[43] The subaltern historians explain the resistance of subalterns located in "...a long tradition of exploitation, or a shorter-term economic dislocation, which provokes resistance and rebellion: challenges to landlords or the agents of the state, the appropriation or destruction of the signs and instruments of their authority. This action, which independently generated and pursued, draws on the insurgents' own original culture for its values, symbols and its means of organising."[44]

How is resistance suppressed? In a colonial situation, the colonial state had the power of defining what constituted opposition to its authority. Therefore, in a colonial situation, the dominance of colonial state was overwhelmingly experienced by the colonised, particularly the subaltern classes, which remain the core aspect of contested political process. The dominance of elites, be they landlords, zamindars, capitalists and money lenders vis-à-vis tenants, landless peasants, workers and the hapless bonded or indebted peasants and labourers were yet other sites of political and social contest or spaces of domination strengthened and abetted strongly by colonial state. The dominance of upper castes vis-à-vis the lower castes and the male dominance vis-à-vis female are also most important sites of contested social terrain. It is these multiple forces of dominance, which engender the myriad forms of resistance among the subalterns in colonial India. Therefore, the domination and resistance at the individual or group level constitute a core and redefining aspect of contested social process. Therefore, dominance and resistance have "a cyclical relationship: domination leads to resistance, which leads to the further exercise of power, provoking further resistance, and so on."[45]

In India, what the colonial State symbolised was the "political domination of a foreign State."[46] The colonial State which gained political dominance through coercion had subsequently encountered a series of resolute resistance from the colonised in India. The Colonial State was thus formed in the crucible of resistance. The resistance of the oppressed against the multiple forms of exploitation by colonial, landlord and capitalist masters has thus a long tradition. So, throughout the period of British colonial rule in India, the process of interrogating and confronting the existing and also emerging social, religious, political, economic, and cultural systems, had become manifest in the varied forms, i.e., in the form of the social and religious reform movements, the popular revolt of 1857 by Indian sepoys and many tribal, peasant and working class struggles throughout the late eighteenth century, through nineteenth century to the second half of the twentieth century. The tradition of resistance and protest was thus not sporadic in the history of colonial India.[47]

## Against the Colonial State: The Revolt of 1857

The first half of the nineteenth century India was significant, primarily for two remarkable developments. First, it represented an era of expansion of British colonialism; second, it witnessed a very fierce defiance from different strata of Indian society. The British attempts at altering the fundamental contours of social, political and economic landscape of India had engendered a series of resolute acts of popular defiance and resistance, which were nevertheless suppressed ruthlessly, demonstrated the rising anti-colonial ideas and assertions of Indian people. The assertions of Indian people, spanned across diverse sections, i.e., subalterns to the disposed landed gentry[48] and different locations, Bengal province to Madras province, became a familiar feature of the period of the British colonial "rapacity"[49] before 1857.

The perceptions of resistance vary depending on the context in which resistance was organised. Hence, the resistance against the British colonial order by different classes of India in 1857 did constitute an act of resistance against the colonial order in the wider meaning, be it by the feudal elements supported by subaltern forces. If the resistance against the British colonial authority had acquired any historical import, it ought to be necessarily interpreted as the remarkable anti-colonial event, threatening the uprooting of colonial control. The 1857 Revolt represented the undaunted expression of anti-colonial spirit or incipient nationalist spirit, of Indians cutting across different social strata against the onslaught of the British colonial rule. A major event, which apparently inspired, fashioned and promoted the ideas of nationalism in colonial India, the other anti-colonial struggles, which occurred in different locations and at different points in time, are crucial to be discoursed for their significance to the project of anti-colonial struggle. The 1857 Revolt continued to remain 'a symbol of popular resistance' against an alien rule. It signified the collective gesture of defiance and the demonstration of strong will of Indians to challenge the oppressive order of British Raj. It could be argued that the 1857 Revolt symbolised the finale of the earlier resistance movements in different locations.

This process of resistance signified blistering protest against the prevailing regimes of dominance and the emerging value systems. The struggles articulated the growing or failed aspirations of diverse social groups representing varied identities like caste, class or gender. The resistance movements by the critical interrogation and intervention in colonial India threw a very serious challenge to the hegemony of Colonial State and other hegemonic socio-cultural practices.

## Colonial State V/s Peasantry

The impact of British colonial rule on Indian society has not been uniform. Diverse social classes responded in varied ways to demonstrate the resistance to the penetration of British colonialism. Colonialism necessarily produces its own resistance. This becomes perceptible, when agrarian economy was in the midst of strained phase of transformation. The communities affected by the development chose to defy the Colonial State. There are two basic theories of peasant rebellions viz., the structural and the historical. The structural explanations focus on different systems of class relationships; the historical explanations focus on the increasing economic insecurity of peasantry engendered by transition to modern world.[50] It is perhaps the latter explanation which is most germane to comprehend the peasant rebellions or revolts that were set in motion against the British during the process of colonisation of India. The scholars of historical theories stressed on the "social discontinuities created by the transition to the modern world."[51] The chief element of historical explanation is that the "peasant grievances centre on increasing economic insecurity."[52] It is this universe of economic insecurity, engendered among the peasant communities which become the raison d'être of peasant revolt.

The antagonistic British colonial regime engendered fierce resistance from peasant communities, disrupting the traditional agrarian set up.[53] With its policy of promoting commercial agriculture and market economy, and replacing the traditional agrarian social setup or 'destruction of pre-or non-capitalist form of social organisation'[54] and construction in its place a new capitalistic agrarian social order,[55] it had adequately provided the necessary conditions for explosion of peasant resistance or rebellions throughout the period of colonial rule in India.[56] The British colonial rule in its project to 'expand the process of colonial extraction from the agrarian sector'[57] restructured the agrarian social order. It created multiple sites of agrarian unrest, which remained throughout the colonial period uninterrupted and unresolved. The Colonial State had only furthered the agrarian social discontent, brewing as a result of tumultuous transformation in the agrarian economy. The discounted peasants had risen against the exploitation of the native landlords/estate holders and displayed their anger against the failure to remove the sources of exploitation, abetting the exploitative classes. The agrarian struggles were just not anti-landlord but also anti-colonial.[58] The peasant struggles were against the 'British encroachment of rights on land, enhancement of revenue rates, statutory landlordism, for better wages and service conditions'. The core issue of the anti-colonial struggle was the agrarian question and focal issue of the agrarian question was the peasants' right to land and labour.[59]

## Colonial State V/s Working Class

The anti-colonial assertions of different social classes are crucial in combating Colonial State. The emerging social classes, particularly the subalterns, awakened to their historic role in the fight against the 'alien' power, questioned the legitimacy of Colonial State. The subaltern agency had become critically significant in the anti-colonial articulations agitation against the imposition of the Rowlatt Act. The subaltern interventions in the successive anti-colonial confrontations during 1920-22, 1930-34, and 1942 frightened the Colonial State, which subsequently deployed the most repressive machinery to throttle the surging tide of subaltern militancy.

In a colonial country like India, there was an inexorable antagonism between the Colonial State and the industrial working class. This antagonism became sharper as the formidable State supported capitalists, whether European or Indian, more forcefully by operating highly inimical and intimidating policy to curb the working class struggles.

The laws, enacted to restrain the expression of resistance, and the institution of police force constituted the core elements of repressive apparatus. The Colonial State brought about several repressive laws to rein in the militancy of working class. It used the police force very often to terrorise industrial workers and break their strikes. These factors have strongly influenced the development of radicalism among industrial workers and formed the raison d'être for their defiance.

The most repressive measures enacted in the form of the Rowlatt Act in 1919, the Trade Disputes Act of 1929, The Public Safety Bill in 1929 were designed to contain the rising working class militancy. The Rowlatt Act in 1919 was enacted to suppress the rising militancy of Indians including the industrial workers and the Public Safety Bill and the Trade Disputes Bill to check the growing revolutionary consciousness of industrial workers and their identification with the anti-colonial struggle. The Meerut Conspiracy Case on March 20, 1929 was launched against 31 labour leaders, most of whom were communists, to contain the growing radicalism among the workers. The section 144 of Criminal Procedure Code, The Unlawful Instigation Ordinance, The Prevention of Molestation and Boycott Ordinance, and the Unlawful Association Ordinance were effectively used against the working class freezing their involvement and solidarity with the movement in various provinces.[60] The industrial working class demonstrated its resentment against the existence of Colonial State by expressing its solidarity with the INA and with RIN mutiny. The Colonial State stands delegitimised to the industrial working class.

**Colonial State V/s Tribes**

The early British anthropologists constructed an ideal type of tribe, as socially homogenous unit having its own dialect, political and cultural institutions and territory isolated from outside influences.[61] Indian society was considered earlier as big laboratory for ethnological research of colonial science. Consequently, the ethnographic discourse on Indian castes and tribes resulted in hierarchical classification. Indian people were merely slotted into different categories on their physical characteristics, habits and socio-economic and cultural advancement.[62] The colonial imperatives and racial prejudices crept into the colonial scientific imagination. Indian people appeared to be low in their social, economic and cultural achievement. The colonial observers beliefs tribals or *Adivasis* were yet to witness the dawn of civilisation.

From the earlier times down to contemporary period, the habitations of tribes are not exclusively confined to few localities or provinces. They are dotted across various regions and terrains.[63] The existence and the struggle to maintain socio-cultural world have been well attested in Indian literature and history.[64] However, the specificity of tribal world has remained an inscrutable concept to colonisers, who developed prejudiced theories classifying aboriginal communities as 'barbaric' or uncivilised.[65] This mode of pigeonholing of certain communities, who for several historical reasons remained or were kept out of developmental discourse, fits in ingeniously with colonisers agenda of civilising mission in the colonised territories.[66] The nineteenth century perception of tribe suggested the particular 'type of society' and the particular 'stage of evolution'. According to this perception, the tribe was isolated, self contained and primitive social formation.[67] The understanding of the tribe in evolutionary mode emphasised their less advanced stage and primitive condition.

The colonial system disrupted traditional social set up of the communities and undermined their economic system by bringing it into contact with the system of market.[68] Thus "with the market came the middle men, merchants and money lenders."[69] The colonial interventionist policies principally made them restive[70] and mobilised tribal resistance in diverse locations[71] of India. The initial phase (1795-1860) coincided with 'the rise, expansion and the establishment of British Empire' in India. K.S. Singh explains:[72]

> "It was resistance to the new system and to the new classes of the people who were inducted by it, namely, the system of local administration and taxation, evangelisation and humanitarian measures, the new landlords, moneylenders and government officials, all of whom were to be thrown out in a violent upsurge. This formulation generally applies to all the movements of this period; the Chuar rebellions (1795-1800), the risings of Chero zamindars and disturbances in Chotanagpur in 1820, the Kol and Bhumij insurrections, the resistance offered by Gond zamindars in 1819 and 1842, and the Konds' resistance to the abolition of the Meriah sacrifice from the mid-1830s. This phase culminated in the Indian Mutiny of 1857, which saw the Chero and Gond zamindars revolt, while many other tribes kept out of it."

The second phase of tribal resistance (1860-1920) had coincided with the intense phase of colonial system, distinguished by deeper penetration of the moneylenders, merchant capital, and the higher incidence of colonial interference.[73] The tribal movements acquired "a curious mix of agrarian, religious and political issues."[74] The prominent movements of the phase were:[75]

> "Santhal Insurrection by the Kharwar movement (1871-80) and the Munda-Oraon Sardar movement (1869-95) by Birsa Munda's and Tana Bhagats' reformative movements (1895-1921), which threw up the charismatic and 'divinely-inspired' brand of leadership. Birsa Munda among the Mundas (1895-1901), Sidhu, Kanhu, Bhagirath and Bubu Gossain among the Santhals (1856-57, 1871-90), Jatra Oraon among the Oraons (1915-22), Gobind Giri among the Bhils, organised and led social and political action for the restoration of their rights and 'kingdom', founded cults and expressed through borrowed Hindu and Christian idioms their people's urge for freedom. All ended in violent classes with the authorities. A few rebellions during this period also resulted from the disturbance of the traditional relationship of the tribes with their rulers in Keonjhar and Bastar."

The third phase of tribal resistance (1920-1947) saw the rise of intensified national struggle for freedom of India with active participation of tribes in it under the influence of Gandhi. The Gandhian reconstruction programme aided the process of politicisation of the tribes. The Koyas and Jatapus participated in the guerilla warfare waged by Sitaram Raju in the Rampa region (1922-24) for the freedom of India. The focus of attack was the colonial regime. The agrarian struggle in Bengal, 1946-47, was marked by the participation of the Santhal peasants. The Warlis of Thana were very well organised to demand the redress of their grievances in the mid-1940s.[76] The tribal communities under the weight of the colonial system and persistent interference into their life pattern lost the unique character. They were transformed by colonialism, but in a far more profound sense than known so far.[77] The colonial system engendered conditions which forced tribal communities resist the state and the conditions of inescapability and helplessness[78] triggering on to intense turbulence and resistance against the state.

## References

1. Aimé Césaire, *'Discourse on Colonialism'*, Trans. Joan Pinkham, New York, Monthly Review Press, 1972, p. 2.
2. S.P. Huntington, *'The Class of Civilisations and the Remaking of World Order'*, New York, Simon and Schuster, 1996, p. 51.
3. Robert. J.C. Young, *White Mythologies: Writing History and the West*, Routledge, London, 2004, p. 1; see also Jenny Sharpe, 'The Violence of Light in the Land of Desire; Or, How William Jones Discovered India', *Boundary* 2, Vol. 20, No. 1. (Spring, 1993), pp. 26-46.
4. Abhjijt Banerjee and Lakshmi Iyer, 'History Institutions and Economic Performance: The Legacy of Colonial and Land Tenure Systems in India', *The American Economic Review*, Vol. 95, No. 4. (Sep., 2005), p. 1190; Note: For an analysis of the role of Colonialism in Economic and social development, see also 'Colonialism and Development: A Comparative Analysis of Spanish and British Colonies' by Matthew Lange, James Mahoney and Matthias vom Hau, *American Journal of Sociology*, Volume 111, Number 5, (March 2006): 1412–62.
5. Partha Chatterjee, *The Partha Chatterjee Omnibus*, (New Delhi, 1999), p. 26 and 33; Robert J.C. Young, *Postcolonialism: An Historical Introduction,* (Oxford, 2001), pp. 4, 6, 7, 15.

6. Bipan Chandra, *Presidential address, A.P. History Congress, XVI session.* Karimnagar, *1992*, p. 8 and 21.
7. Andre Gunder Frank, 'India in the World Economy, 1400-1750', *Economic and Political Weekly*, Vol. 31, No. 30 (July 27, 1996), p. 50.
8. *Ibid.*, p. 54.
9. Bharat Patankar and Gail Omvedt, 'The Bourgeois State in Post-Colonial Social Formation', *Economic and Political Weekly*, Vol. 12, No. 53 (Dec. 31, 1977), p. 2172.
10. Eugene F. Irschick, 'Order and Disorder in Colonial South India', *Modern Asian Studies*, Vol. 23, No. 3 (1989), p. 459; Note: Colonialism ... "was a system of exploitation of people of a geographically defined area with definite ethic and cultural characteristics by an alien group which was ethnically and culturally distinct and which did not regard India as a home.", see Amiya Kumar Bagchi, Colonialism and the Nature of 'Capitalist' Enterprise in India', *Economic and Political Weekply,* Vol. 23, No. 31 (July. 3, 1988), PE-45.
11. Note: "The idea of Britain being an imperial people, with the mission of civilising backward people, had a deep root, it had its origin in the conquest of Ireland." See For a critical analysis of Colonial attitudes toward the colonised space, Biplab Dasgupta, 'The Colonial Political Perspective,' *Social Scientist*, Vol. 3. No. 3/4. (March – April, 2003), p. 30.
12. Tapan Raychaudhuri, *Perceptions, Emotions, Sensibilities: Essays on India's Colonial and Post-colonial Experiences*, Oxford University Press, New Delhi, p.164.
13. N. Ram, 'Impact of Early Colonisation on Economy of South India', *Social Scientist,* Vol. I, No. 4, November, 1972, pp. 59-62; Also see Irfan Habib's 'Colonisation of the Indian Economy, 1757-1900' *Social Scientist*, pp. 23-53.
14. Bharat Patankar and Gail Omvedt, *op.cit*, p. 2171.
15. Note: 'India came to be described as a vast pathological reservoir, "overlaid perennially by a thick layer of maladies". The new 'code words' were sudden, severe, decline, decadence, deterioration, degeneration and the worst,

putrefaction'; See Deepak Kumar, 'Medical Encounter in British India, 1820-1920', *Economic and Political Weekly*, Vol. 32, No. 4 (Jan. 25-31, 1997), p. 166; Also see Ronald Inden's 'Orientalist Constructions of India', *Modern Asian Studies*, Vol. 20, No. 3 (1986), pp. 401-446.

16. David Scott, 'Colonial Governmentality', *Social Text*, No. 43 (Autumn), 1995, p. 192.
17. Rosalind O'Hanlon, Recovering the Subject Subaltern Studies and Histories of Resistance in Colonial South Asia', *Modern Asian Studies*, Vol. 22, No. 1 (1988), p. 217.
18. David Scott, *op.cit.*, p. 205.
19. See Jenny Sharpe, 'The Violence of Light in the Land of Desire; Or, How William Jones Discovered India', *Boundary* 2, Vol. 20, No. 1. (Spring, 1993), pp. 26-46.
20. Ranajit Guha, 'Dominance without hegemony: history and power in colonial India', Harvard University Press, 1997, p. 155.
21. See Claude Marcovits, 'Some Trends in European (Mainly British) Historiography of Modern India', *Economic and Political Weekly*, Vol. 22, No. 10 (Mar. 7, 1987), pp. 416-418; See also S. Bhattacharya, Paradigms Lost: Notes on Social History in India, *Economic and Political Weekly*, Vol. 17, No. 14/16, Annual Number, (Apr., 1982), pp. 690-693+695-696.; also see Eugene F. Irschick, 'Order and Disorder in Colonial South India', pp. 460-461 and 476-480 .
22. Deepak Kumar, 'Medical Encounter in British India, 1820-1920', p. 166.
23. Ann Stoler, 'Perceptions of Protest: Defining the Dangerous in Colonial Sumatra', *American Ethnologist*, Vol. 12, No. 4 (Nov., 1985), p. 648.
24. Alastair Pennycook, *op.cit.*, p. 35; See also Frederick Cooper, 'Decolonising Situations: The Rise, Fall, and Rise of Colonial Studies, 1951-2001', *French Politics, Culture and Studies*, Vol. 20. 2002.
25. Note: They advanced the idea that Indians knew of "no rights and democracy" and were always under authoritarian rule.

Thus early history of despotism in India had been churned out as a justification for imposition on Indians a despotic colonial state; See Biplab Dasgupta, *op.cit.*, p. 30; Note: 'The agenda of colonialism was conquest, rule and administration, and not the activity of writing histories, although many administrators did write histories.' The use of expressions such as "uncultivated minds', 'perfectly destitute of historical records' to refer to Indians and their sense of history disclose the colonisers prejudiced perception of Indian people. See 'Temporalities, History and Routines of Rule in Colonial India' by U. Kalpagam, *Time and Society*, 1999, Vol. 8 (1): pp. 144 and 146.

26. S. Srinivasa Raghavaiyangar, Memorandum on the Progress of the Madras Presidency during the last forty years of British Administration, (Madras, 1893), New Delhi, Asian Educational Services, 1988, p. 25; See also Dua, J.C., 'Nature of the Poligar Revolts in the Ceded Districts during the First Half of the Nineteenth Century,' *Proceedings of the 35th Session of Indian History Congress*, Jadavpur (Calcutta), 1974, p. 235.

27. J.D.B. Gribble, A Manual of the District of Cuddapah in the Presidency of Madras, Madras, (Govt Press), 1875, 132-134; Note: A critical interrogation of colonial construction of native space: " In this essay I focus on the manner in which aesthetics and colonial ideology imbricate in early descriptions of Indian landscape. I argue that 18th century aesthetics of the sublime furnished a ready tool with which the traveller articulated specifically colonial themes in her/ his narrative. My concern is the rhetorical transformation of the Indian landscape from the site of sublime desolation and danger to potential improvement in the 1750-1820 period. The aesthetics of sublime, common to 18th century Europe embodies terror and vastness, darkness and obscurity, danger and challenge. What is interesting is that this rhetorical transformation of India cuts across many different kinds of English writing – travelogues, administrative reports, letters from officials, memoirs and so on. That is, there appears to be an entire discourse in operation here,

as I shall demonstrate using sample texts from these genres." Pramod. K. Nayar, 'The Sublime Raj: English Writing and India, 1750-1820,' *Economic and Political Weekly*, August 21, 2004; Note: 'Each new institution, regulation or practice that the colonial government sought to introduce was legitimised as an attempt to bring 'order' to what was in the past seemingly disorderly.', See U. Kalpagam, 'Temporalities, History and Routines of Rule in Colonial India', op.cit., p. 154.

28. Jyotsna G. Singh, *Colonial Narratives / Cultural Dialogues: Discoveries of India in the Language of Colonialism*, Routledge, New York, 1996, p. 3.

29. Note: The other considerations, which also guided the British to introduce the systems of land tenure, were to promote the trade, to satisfy the hunger of Britain's burgeoning capitalist class for markets, and also enhance the land revenue on a sustained basis; See D. Subramanyam Reddy, 'Changing Agrarian Relations and State of Peasantry in Andhra During Early Nineteenth Century,' *Social Scientist*, Vol. 14, No. 6, (Jun., 1986), p. 33.

30. See for an elaborate explanation and review of the works on the concept of 'Resistance', Jocelyn A. Hollander and Rachel L. Einwohner, 'Conceptualising Resistance', *Sociological Forum*, Vol. 19, No. 4 (Dec., 2004), pp. 533-554.

31. Rosalind O'Hanlon, op.cit, p. 215.

32. Mridula Mukherjee, Peasant Resistance and Peasant Consciousness in Colonial India: 'Subalterns' and Beyond', *Economic and Political Weekly*, Vol. 23, No. 41 (Oct. 8, 1988), p. 2114.

33. David Scott, 'Colonial Governmentality', p. 192.

34. Robert J.C. Young, *Postcolonialism: A Historical Introduction,* (Oxford, 2001), p. 161 and 163; Susantha Goonetilake, "Colonial Culture" *Social Scientist,* Vol. 4, No. 42, January 1976, p. 35; Bipan Chandra, *India's Struggle for Independence*, New Delhi, 1989, Chapter 17, 210 to 223; Frederick Cooper, Conflict and Connection: Rethinking

Colonial African History', *The American Historical Review*, Vol. 99, No. 5, (Dec., 1994), p. 1520 and 1532.

35. David Featherstone, 'Spacialities of Transnational Resistance to Globalisation: The Maps of Grievance of the Inter-Continental Caravan', *Transactions of the Institute of British Geographers*, New Series, Vol. 28, No. 4 (Dec., 2003), p. 405.
36. David Featherstone, p. 408.
37. Rosalind O'Hanlon, *op.cit*, p. 216.
38. Susan Bibler Coutin and Susan F. Hirsch, 'Naming Resistance: Ethnographers, Dissidents, and States', *Anthropological Quarterly*, Vol. 71. No.1 (Jan., 1998), p. 1.
39. Jocelyn A. Hollander and Rachel L. Einwohner, *op. cit.*, p. 534.
40. *Ibid.,* p. 538.
41. James C. Scott, *Weapons of the Weak: Everyday Forms of Peasant Resistance*, OUP, Delhi, 1990, p. xvi.
42. *Ibid.,* p. xvii.
43. Note: "Historical-structural" approaches "show ideology, values, traditions, and rituals to be of consequence and trace the importance of culture to group, organisation, and community dynamics and to other features of social structure. Yet they never presume that protest is mechanically determined by social structure. They show the patterning of defiance to be contingent on historical circumstance.", Eckstein S, ed. *Power and Popular Protest: Latin American Social Movements*, Berkeley, University of California Press, 1989, p. 3, quoted in Marc Edelman, ' Social Movements: Changing Paradigms and Forms of Politics', *Annual Review of Anthropology*, Vol. 30 (2001), p. 291.
44. Rosalind O'Hanlon, *op.cit.*, p. 213.
45. Jocelyn A. Hollander and Rachel L. Einwohner, *op. cit.*, p. 548.
46. Bharat Patankar and Gail Omved, *op.cit.*, p. 2171.
47. L.S. Vishwanath, 'Peasant Movements in Colonial India: An Examination of Some Conceptual Frameworks',

*Economic and Political Weekly*, Vol. 25, No. 2 (Jan. 13, 1990), pp. 118-122.

48. Dua, J.C., *op. cit.*, p. 235.
49. See for classical characterisation and description of the British rule in India, Karl Marx and Engels, *The First War of Independence, 1857-59*, Progress Publishers, Moscow, 34, 1975, quoted in Bisvamoy Pati, Historians and Historiography: Situating 1857, 12 May, 2007, *Economic and Political Weekly*, pp. 1686-91.
50. See for a critical analysis of theories on peasant rebellions in the modern era; J. Craig Jenkins, 'Why do Peasants Rebel? Structural and Historical Theories of Modern Peasant Rebellions,' *The American Journal of Sociology*, Vol. 88, No. 3. (Nov. 1988)., pp. 487-514.
51. *Ibid.*, p. 490.
52. *Ibid*; Note: Craig writes: 'Broadly speaking, there have been two historical formulations – the "market" theory advanced by Hobsbawm (1959), Wolf (1969), Migdal (1974), and Chirot and Ragin (1975). Both versions argue that peasant grievances center on increasing economic insecurity – the market theory by pointing to the sharp fluctuations of a market economy and the exploitation theory to the increasing economic exactions of landowners and the state; Also see Daniel Chirot; Charles Ragin, 'The Market, Tradition and Peasant Rebellion: The Case of Romania in 1907', *American Sociological Review*, Vol. 40, No. 4. (Aug., 1975), pp. 428-444.
53. S.K. Mittal; Kapil Kumar, 'Anti-Feudal and Anti-Colonial Struggles of the Oudh Peasantry in Early 1920s', *Social Scientist*, Vol. 8, No. 12. (Jul., 1980), p. 28.
54. Alastair Pennycook, *English and the Discourses of Colonialism*, Routledge, London, 1998, p. 37.
55. Note: 'While the quantum and mode of revenue payment allowed the colonial state to insert itself into the 'lived' and 'working' times of the peasantry, the working hours of the peasantry and the agricultural laborers were never directly

regulated by the state.' U. Kalpagam, *'Temporalities, History and Routines of Rule in Colonial India' op.cit.*, pp. 146-47.

56. Note: 'This evolution of the legal structure of landed property, and the specific role in it of the colonial state, must, of course, be seen in the context of an agrarian economy increasingly dominated by the fact of "commercialisation", because this was the specific form of the expanding process of colonial appropriation in British India from the second half of the nineteenth century', See Partha Chatterjee, 'Colonial State and Peasant Resistance in Bengal 1920-1947' *Past and Present*, No. 110 (Feb., 1986), p. 176.
57. *Ibid.*, p. 186.
58. See for a critical analysis of Peasant Movements in Colonial India, L. S. Vishwanath, 'Peasant Movements in Colonial India: An Examination of Some Conceptual Frameworks', *Economic and Political Weekly*, Vol. 25, No. 2 (Jan. 13, 1990), pp. 118-122.
59. K.C. Suri, 'The Agrarian Question in India during the National Movement, 1885-1947', *Social Scientist*, Vol. 15, No. 10 (Oct., 1987), p. 25.
60. See K. Venugopal Reddy, *Class Colonialism and Nationalism*, (New Delhi, 2002) pp. 66-68 and *Working Class and Freedom Struggle*, 1918-22, (New Delhi, 2005) p. 60.
61. Vidyut Joshi, (ed), *Tribal Situation in India: Issues in Development; with special reference to Western India*, (Rawat Publications), Jaipur and New Delhi, 1998), p. 16.
62. Note: 'What was happening in the forestry sector was to some extent a manifestation of the larger Orientalist colonial project of constructing India as knowable by representation... While forest dwellers were being sorted into types by tribe and caste, the forests themselves were arranged in categories by dominant genera and species. Such description and the laying down of taxonomic structures to

represent biotic communities presaged colonial development projects in which human and natural resources were harnessed for imperial purposes.' See K. Sivaramakrishnan, 'Colonialism and Forestry in India: Imagining the Past in Present Politics', *Comparative Studies in Society and History*, Vol. 37, No. 1. (Jan., 1995), p. 6.

63. Devendra Thakur and D.N. Thakur, (ed), *Tribal Life and Forests: Tribal Life in India* (Deep and Deep Publications, New Delhi), 1994.

64. A.L. Basham, *The Wonder that was India*, Rupa and Co, New Delhi, 1984, pp.199-200.

65. K.S. Singh, 'Colonial Transformation of Tribal Society in Middle India' *Economic and Political Weekly,* Vol. 13, No. 30 (July. 29, 1978), p.1221.

66. Biswamoy Pati, pp. vii to ix. and Meena Radhakrishna, pp.1-23. Biswamoy Pati, (January 2006), 'Editorial Note', *The Indian Historical Review*, Vol. XXXIII, No. 1, pp. vii to ix; Meena Radhakrishna, (January 2006), see for colonial constructions of identity of Aboriginals in colonial India, 'Of Apes and Ancestors: Evolutionary Science and Colonial Ethnography', *The Indian Historical Review*, Vol. XXXIII, No. 1, pp.1-23.

67. André Béteille, (April., 1998), 'The Idea of Indigenous People', *Current Anthropology*, Vol. 39. No. 2, pp. 186-187.

68. Note: 'It is by now well established that the imperatives of colonial forestry were essentially commercial. Its operations were dictated more by the commercial and strategic utility of different species than by broader social or environmental considerations.' See Ramachandra Guha and Madhav Gadgil, 'State Forestry and Social Conflict in British India' *Past and Present*, No. 123. (May, 1989), p. 144.

69. K.S. Singh, 'Colonial Transformation of Tribal Society in Middle India' *op.cit.*, p.1227.

70. *Note:* (a) 'In the early decades of its rule, the colonial state was markedly indifferent to forest conservancy. Until well

into the nineteenth century, forests were viewed by administrators as an impediment to the expansion of cultivation. With the state committed to agricultural expansion as its major source of revenue, the early decades of colonial rule witnessed a "fierce onslaught" on India's forest. The first show of interest in forestry -the reservation of teak forests in Malabar in 1806 -was dictated by strategic imperial needs.' Further, (b) '... state monopoly over forests was safeguarded by the stringent provisions of the Indian Forest Act of 1878. This was a comprehensive piece of legislation -later to serve as a model for other British colonies -which by one stroke of the executive pen attempted to obliterate centuries of customary use of the forest by rural populations all over India.' (c) 'Thus when the colonial state asserted control over woodland which had earlier been in the hands of local communities, and proceeded to work these forests for commercial timber production, it intervened in the day to day life of the Indian villager to an unprecedented degree.' See Ramachandra Guha and Madhav Gadgil, 'State Forestry and Social Conflict in British India' *op.cit.*, pp. 144, 145 and 147.

71. *Note:* 'In the context of colonial societies like India, colonialism imposed new realities that threatened to decimate the adibasi population.' See Biswamoy Pati, 'Survival as Resistance: Tribals in Colonial Orissa', *The Indian Historical Review*, Vol. XXXIII, No. 1 (January 2006), p.175.

72. K.S. Singh, 'Colonial Transformation of Tribal Society in Middle India' *op.cit.*, pp. 1229-30.

73. *Note:* 'The 'Modern' sector impacted on tribal society by undermining their existence. ...Besides, the price of being wrenched to the world capitalist system implied that other oppressive features associated with the internal order of exploitation were systematically reinforced. These were related to coercive extractions that ranged from forced labour (*bethi* and *goti*) and the forcible supply of provisions (*gudam*, as it was called in the Jeypur zamindari) to crippling tax burdens which left them at the mercy of the moneylenders,

the princely rulers and the zamindars...Colonial capitalism also joined in to exploit the tribals.' See Biswamoy Pati, 'Survival as Resistance' pp.194-195.

74. K.S. Singh, 'Colonial Transformation of Tribal Society in Middle India' *op.cit.*, p. 1230.

75. *Ibid.*

76. *Ibid.*

77. *Note*: 'It has been suggested that British colonial rule marks an important watershed in the ecological history of India. The encounter with a technologically advanced and dynamic culture gave rise to profound dislocations at various levels of Indian society.' See Ramachandra Guha and Madhav Gadgil, 'State Forestry and Social Conflict in British India' *op.cit.*, p. 142. Also note: 'Perhaps what needs to be emphasised is that the combined might of the 'old' and 'new' barely left the tribals in a position to survive. This was contested through the anti-colonial / feudal mass movements over 1920-1947 period.' See Biswamoy Pati, 'Survival as Resistance' *op.cit.*, p. 175.

78. Note: The Baigas' tribe small tribe of the Mandla, Balaghat and Bilaspur districts of the present day Madhya Pradesh, in petition submitted to the British government in 1892 lamented the loss of their livelihood and miserable conditions into which they were thrown after *Jhum* cultivation was stopped. It states: '..."We daily starve, having had no food grain in our possession. The only wealth we possess is our axe. We have no clothes to cover our body with, but we pass cold nights by the fireside. We are now dying for want of food. We cannot go elsewhere, as the British government is everywhere. What fault have we done that the government does not take care of us? Prisoners are supplied with ample food in jail. A cultivator of the grass is not deprived of his holding, but the Government does not give us our right who have lived here for generations past".

See Ramachandra Guha and Madhav Gadgil, 'State Forestry and Social Conflict in British India' *op.cit.*, p. 153.

# 7

# Colonialism, Emergence of Capital and Labour in Colonial Orissa 1900-1947

*Manoj Kumar Sahoo*

Many scholars have the notion that in the colonial period, the province of Orissa (then the part of Bengal Presidency till 1912 and Bihar till 1936) was not industrialised. The development of industry and the process of industrialisation does not mean only large scale heavy industries, but also refers to the small scale industries like cottage and handicraft industries. An attempt is being made to present the process of capital formation, industrialisation and growth of industrial labour force in colonial Orissa.

The industrial revolution in England brought British imperialism to India in the latter part of eighteenth century. Then India became, what Lord Curzon claimed for the critics of British rule during the debate on the budget for 1901-02, "the brightest jewel in the British Crown".[1] There were many changes in the field of trade and industry, which affected the economic life of Indians.

So, one of the most momentous and negative consequences of British supremacy in India was the disruption of centuries old "union between agriculture and manufacturing industry". As a result, there was a decline and destruction of the Indian town handicraft and village artisan industries. The positive aspect of British rule in India was development of modern industry. The process of industrialisation developed gradually in India, though at the initial stage in major provinces followed by all the provinces.[2]

Orissa province which was part of Bengal Presidency was less industrialised than other provinces. It could not industrialise despite huge amounts of deposited raw materials and cheap labour force. It is interesting to note Haribanbhu Mohanty's conversation with one of the prominent industrialists (*An Industrial Survey of Orissa*) where in he said that an industry requires raw materials, power, labour, and market, but Orissa does not have power, making any industrialist back out.[3]

Orissa was famous for cottage industries and textile industry. These industries met requirements of villagers earlier. Many of the south-eastern and some European countries endorsed its image.[4] The Europeans fully acknowledged the calicoes of Balasore, Bhadrak, Harispur and Hariharpur. Fine muslin of Gulnagar in Kendra Para sub-division in Cuttack district had good reputation within and outside India. Besides, cotton of coarse variety were made in villages for local use. Sometimes, the products of weaving were not merely sold in localities, but were sent to *haats* (local market).[5] Cottage industries were the backbone of economic development of the masses employed for half time in the agriculture. The industry suffered from lack of support from organisation, finance and competition from foreign as well as large scale Indian producers. The artisans confined to villages were engaged in supplying the needs of the agricultural population. They seldom were acquainted with modern process and efficient production and application of labour saving devices, without skills to utilise raw materials cheaper production. The uses of improved applications were unknown to most of them.[6]

The prominant indigenous industries were Weaving Textile Industry, Metal Industry, Brass and Bell Industry, Filigree Industry, Rope Industry, Food and Allied Industry, Paper Industry, Sugar Industry, Glass and Ceramic Industry, Silk Weaving Industry, Hide Industry, Stone Caraving Industry, Sugar Factory at Aska, Rum Factory at Aska, Carpentry Industry, Fisheries, Mrudanga Industry, and so on, which depended on the internal and external trade. The availability of raw materials at lower cost, communication facilities, the currency system and the competition among finished goods available have tremendous impact on the prosperity and continuity of the industries. Lack of market, communication facilities, declining portal trade, the monopolistic nature of British trade, natural disasters like great famine of 1866, foreign as well as Indian goods competition, kept their identity at stake up to early 20th century.

**Development of Industries**

People of Orissa had not seen the mechanised industries till the beginning of the 20th century. Neither the British government nor any British company was interested to start the mechanised industries in the province, where the British administration tried to completely wreck the cottage and small-scale industries to monopolise the market through machine made goods. The opening of the railway lines by the end of the 19th century gave a fillip to the industry,[7] when some native industrialist, Utkal Gaurab Madhusudhan Das, took initiatiave to do so.

## Utkal Gaurab Madhusudan Das and Industrialisation in Orissa

Madhusudan Das was one of the pioneers, who played a very significant role in shaping the economic prosperity of Orissa through industries.[8] He actively encouraged local handicrafts and cottage industries. He had made serious attempt to revitalise the languishing cottage industries in the province. He had promoted the idea of Swadeshi in Orissa even before the Swadeshi movement began in Bengal. For his tireless contribution to the economic development of Orissa, he was popularly known as *"Kulabruddha"*.[9] The idea of pioneering Swadeshi movement was conceived before to the partition of Bengal by him.[10] He introduced *Charkha* (spinning wheel) and encouraged cotton cultivation for production of Swadeshi goods by establishing Orissa Art Wares and the Utkal Tannery in Orissa, in general, and in Cuttack, in particular.[11]

### Orissa Art Wares

Madhubabu established the factory of *Orissa Art Wares* in 1899-1900,[12] within his hiring residential premises,[13] a hundred men, engaged in the delicate craft of gold and silver filigree work. It produced fine polish filigree works from gold, silver, aluminum, ivory, besides, producing photo frame, *ataradana*, bowl, beetle box, handle of sticks, bracelet, bangle, armlet, button, anklet, locket and whatnot.[14] In addition, horn, ivory and wood carving, brass, ammonium and many beautiful handicraft products. Madhubabu introduced new methods in remodelling the work structure and taught workers to produce articles matching the modern taste, which were admired even by the high ranking British officers. These include, W. Weden Burn, Charles Elliot, I.E Webster, Maddox, U.S. Club, S.N. Banarjee, B.B. Kapur of Bardwan, private secretary to Lt. Governor of Bengal, Wellis Samser, W. Lawrence, E.B Harris, et al. Lt. Governor of Bengal, Sir John Woodburn, visited the Orissa Art Wares, and addressed the audience in Oriya written on a palm leaf artistically ornamented and enclosed in a silver casket of excellent mark bearing miniature figure of Bhubaneswar temple. A similar casket, that was given to Lord Curzon at Puri during his first visit to Orissa in December 1900, was highly appreciated. Often, the factory was well equipped with modern machinery.[15]

Orissa Art Wares was the first organised factory in Orissa started by private enterprises. Madhubabu exhorted the village weavers to come over to his workshop and receive better training in weaving.[16] The finished goods from that factory were exported to Colombo, parts of Asia and Europe through the three major ports, Batighara (Lighthouse) of Cuttack, Chandbali of Balasore and Pipli of Puri. The product at home were in demand in Banaras and elsewhere.[17]

**Utkal Tannery**

The factory of Utkal Tannery was another private financed industry with requisite techniques near Cuttack railway station across about 40 acres of land. Madhubabu invested a considerable amount of money,[18] in producing finished goods using lizard skin and others. In the beginning, the products of lizard skin had great demand in England and America. Madhubabu rejected the goods which lost finishing quality. According to the report of the collector of Cuttack, the leather industry of Madhusudhan Das was an important industry of Orissa ranking No. 5 in the Government shortlisted table. The factory used the skin of crocodiles, serpents and lizards, easily available in Orissa and were collected for the shoe factory at the instance of Madhusudan Das. After preliminary work the factory manufactured fine quality of shoes, which earned good reputation at home and aboard.[19]

In 1908, the government of British India appointed a committee under the chairmanship of Mr. J.G. Cumming to review the industrial position of Bengal. Three factories in Bengal, Bihar and Orissa hiring some fifty workmen or more found importance. The Utkal Tannery was the only tannery which was mentioned in his review. According to Mr. Sachidananda Sinha, the Finance Member in the government of Bihar and Orissa, Utkal Tannery at Cuttack stood as the living monument. Lt. Governor of Bihar and Orissa, his private secretary Mr. C.B. Bagley, Honourable Mr. S. Ali Imman, Law Member, Vice Regal Councils, Sir Ashutosh Mukherjee, Vice Chancellor, Calcutta University, Sir Robert Carlyle, Revenue Member of Viceroy's Executive council, the Hindustan Review. On 19 August 1925, Mahatma Gandhi paid a special visit to the Utkal Tannery at Cuttack and became the guest of Madhusudan for being acquainted with the programmers of Utkal Tannery. By seeing the efforts of Madhusudan Das, Miss Sailabala, the adopted daughter of Mrs. Das, said, "He started several industries at home which ultimately ruined him financially. His aim was to develop the industries of his country so that the workmen would earn more." Madhubabu was a strong advocate of technical education for the growth of industries not only in Orissa but also in India. He advocated for introduction of traditional crafts from the primary standards as well as to impart technical training to Oriya students by sending them abroad with financial support. He played a very significant role in a private and industrial institution at Baripada. For development of communication, he demanded for extension of railway and Chandbali port (Balasore district).[20]

Sri Ganesh Dutt Singh, Minister, Local Self Government of Bihar and Orissa opined about Madhubabu "He was generally generous and charitable. He was very keen on the industrial development of the country, which he considered essential for providing labour to the poor and with this idea; he started "Utkal Tannery" which unfortunately was the cause of his financial ruin. He was keen for its development and he made considerable sacrifice for it. In order to teach shoe making he himself became a "shoemaker". The products of Utkal Tannery excelled the quality of those of other countries abroad. The quality and durability of these products of this factory commanded the use of the goods by even the soldiers during the First World War."[21] Assessing his contribution towards the industrialisation of Orissa, Swami Bichitrananda Das stated, "He emphasised the usefulness of cottage industries, the formation of joint stock companies and co-operative industries as early as 1903. Really, he lived much ahead of his time. He helped and encouraged cotton cultivation to save the people from hard competition with waste and to save the struggling weavers and cultivators in their hard competition with Manchester goods."

Unfortunately, the Utkal Tannery could not survive beyond 1927.[22]

## Cottage Industries

Cottage industries were of great importance for the economic development. But they suffered a serious blow during the last decades of nineteenth century due to the lack of institutional finance and competition from foreign as well as large scale Indian producers. The artisans were generally confined to village and were engaged in supplying the needs of the agriculture production. They were not acquainted with the modern processes of efficient production and the application of labour saving devices. The uses of improved appliances were unknown to most of the artisans.[23]

The cottage industries rejuvenated following the laying down of the East Coast railway line. Formation of Utkal Sammilani in 1903 gave fillip and new shape to the rejuvenation of cottage industries in the province. In its second session, the first step was made by the leaders of Orissa. In this session, the provisions were made for the development of small scale and cottage industries in Orissa. Then the other sessions like third, fourth, seventh, eighth, ninth, fifteenth were the most important sessions in which the provisions for the development of cottage and small scale industries in Orissa were made.[24] But the practical shape was given to the same, with the emergence of new leader and industrialist, Madhusudan Das. All these events gave a new industrial life to the people of Orissa.

## Filigree Work

Cuttack was, and still is known for its filigree work. The gold and silver ornaments, fancy articles, caskets, powder cases, toys etc., were sold in Calcutta, Bombay, and Delhi and also exported to Europe. The articles like wires of silver or gold wing were exquisite in design and delicate in finish, spaking highly of artistic talent of designers and finishers. Some 400 families in the town and 2,000 in the rural areas of the district of Cuttack were engaged in the manufacture of gold and silver ornaments and filigree work. Majority of them were poor, who worked as wage earners, whose artistic production benefit went to outside middle men and merchants efforts were made to establish them in workers union or co-operative societies.[25]

**Horn and Ivory Industry**

The manufacture of horn and ivory articles was another important cottage industry of Orissa. Horn goods owe to buffalo horns, in towns of Cuttack and Paralakhemundi. The articles of Orissa were exported to Bombay, Calcutta and elsewhere. The combs prepared were stronger than imported varieties. Sticks, penholders, paper cutters, toothbrush, sticks, fancy articles and toys were also made from horns.[26]

**Toy Making Industry**

The toy making was an important art. Cuttack was famous for its toys. Clay toys from Cuttack were sold in almost all parts of Orissa and neighbouring provinces. The manufacture of unbreakable toys was an innovation of the core cottage industries. The articles were being sold not only in Orissa but also in the other provinces like Central Provinces, Berar, Bombay and Delhi.[27]

**Cane Work Industry**

Cane industry was also an important industry in Orissa. It was the major cottage industry in twentieth century Orissa, particularly Cuttack and Puri. Although cane grew throughout the districts of Cuttack and Puri, it also grew in other districts of Orissa. Split cane was used in rural areas for tying bamboo framework of thatched roofs beside basket-making. Dampara in Cuttack and Banpur in Puri districts were centres of production where the best varieties of cane grew. The cane seats and back of chairs and settees were woven by nearby workers. The Cuttack Iail, the poor industries and the Madhusudan Village Industries Institute made a variety of cane articles, viz., chairs, tables, baskets, trays.

**Coir Industry**

The coir industry was one of the most important industries in Orissa during the twentieth century. It developed mostly in the coastal districts of Orissa. Coir or coconut fibre is a by-product from coconut crop, in the coastal areas. Jagatsingpur, Kendrapara, Cuttack, Dadar and, Jaipur sub-division of Cuttack,[29] places like Sakhigopal, Pipili, Biragovindapur and Chandanpur, in Puri district, and part of the north Balasore are some of the centres.[30] Orissa stands fourth in the production of mature coconut.[31] Cuttack occupied second position, next to Puri followed by Balasore. The industry was the first developing industry which was managed by both private and co-operative sectors. For this industry, new materials were abundantly available in the coastal district of Orissa such as Cuttack, Puri, Balasore and Ganjam.[32]

It required raw materials like long-staple coir fibre and rubber. These industries also imported raw material from Kerala. After obtaining raw materials like coconut fibre, it was spun into ropes either by hand or on a wheel.

It was made into matting, door mats, mattresses, etc. Considerable quantities of fibre were exported from India to foreign countries. The coconut, its coir and finished goods were exported from Sakhigopal railway to the other parts of India. On an average, about 31 thousand mounds of coconut were sent out from that station alone. The rope making and twine provided livelihood to nearly 4,300 persons in the district of Puri and the same number also in Cuttack.[33]

**Jute Industry**

Jute was one of the most important commercial crop of the province. The modern name for the fibre is derived from the Oriya word *'Jhot' or 'Jhout'*, the name by which the material is generally known in Orissa. Although there was no jute mill in Orissa, but it exported raw jute to other provinces in India. Orissa produced nearly 29,000 tonnes of jute per year during the early part of twentieth century. The chief jute growing areas were in Cuttack district on the bank of the Kendrapara canal. A proposal was made in 1936-37 to establish a jute mill at Cuttack in Orissa to manufacture gunnies, hessians and other jute fabrics. But this plan did not materialise due to the lack of finance and machines. But this proposal again came into being in 1975, when the Konark Jute Mill at Dhanmandal in Cuttack was established. Although colonial Orissa, does not have jute mill, some jute cottage industries were established in Bant, Basudevpur of Balasore. The people made excellent gunny bags for the use of pack bullocks. These handmade gunny bags were more durable than mill made products. Beautiful coloured door mats, durries and staircase runners were also manufactured with jute strings, much cheaper than those made with costly yarns. The small durries could serve the purpose of a bed or a mat for poor villager. Weaving durries was so simple that any villager could weave them at his home.[34]

**Handloom Weaving Industry**

Weaving was the most important small scale industry in Orissa, and it was spread all over the province. The handloom products of Orissa were in great demand not only in Orissa and India but also most of the other countries of the world. The number of looms reported was 50,300 and the weavers approximately 169, 000, who handled some 14.72 million Ibs of yards and wove 14.73 million yards of cloth every year. Some of the cotton weavers exhibited considerable taste in colour and variety of textile goods for which they were highly appreciated. Some weaving centres were famous for artistic designs weaving fabrics, for example, Dhalapathara and Baragard for *purda* or door screens and Ragadi in Banki (Cuttack) for the temple border sari. The screens and table cloths produced were so artistic in design attracting users in Sweden. The weavers couldn't get the yarn, dyes and colours, needed in marketing products, as they were not organised into co-operative societies.

Orissa Handloom Marketing Organisation did a remarkable work, but its activities were rather limited to a few localities.[35] So, the weaving demonstration parties could work by instructing weavers in the use of improved appliances, and approved modern weaving pattern. The Department of Industries and Labour, Government of India, got the Accountant General of Bihar to transfer the sum of Rs. 1,905 to the Government of Orissa for the development of the handloom industries at Cuttack and other places for the year 1935-36.[36] Then the Department of Industry, Government of

India, directed the provincial government to spread the assistance scheme to the development of handloom industry for the period of five years.[37]

Demonstration parties like Cuttack Party and Sambalpur Party introduced 458 fly shuttle looms, 109 dobbies and six warping drums. New designs were introduced and weavers were mobilised to participate in the exhibitions within the province and outside. The Cuttack Demonstration Party introduced 232 improved looms, 57 dobbies three warping sets, 12 pegs warping, 27 double beams, four paddle chakras, 11 durry and newen frame, two double shuttle sleys and two blanket looms. Technical assistance was given to a government institution and to seven small weaving factories, including a carpet factory. Efforts were also made with small success to manufacture improved looms in the villages.[38]

In 1936, for organising weavers organising societies under the market organisation, one organiser and two weaving supervisors were appointed. Three societies were organised by them, two under the Cuttack Central Co-operative Bank. For selling manufactured goods, a sale depot was established where saris and *gamchas* (napkin) were sold. The Central Co-operative Bank was established at Balasore, Bhadrak and Angul.[39] In 1937-38, the annual handloom exhibition was held in the Ravenshaw College campus at Cuttack, in which Cuttack Demonstration Party introduced 229 fly shuttle looms, 25 dobbies and three work drums. Dyeing was conducted by the Cuttack Party at the Orissa Poor Industry Cottage on jute, palm leaf and Palmyra grass. During that year, Orissa[40] received a grant of Rs. 13,400 from the Government of India for the development of the handloom industries in Orissa. During the year 1939-40, four weaving demonstration parties came into being in Orissa. Among them two permanent parties like Cuttack and Sambalpur district, and the two temporary parties one for the district of Ganjam and Koraput and other for Balasore continued to render help to the weavers by introducing different kinds of labour saving appliances and marketable patterns. During that year, for the first time *jackuard* weaving was introduced for weaving elaborate design of sari borders. This helped check, to a certain extent, the impact of sari and other fancy patterns into Orissa. The All India Spinners Association, Utkal branch, received technical help from all the four demonstration parties. The weaving factory at Tura was the biggest one and got technical help from Cuttack Demonstration Party. Apart from that, this party provided technical help to six other institutions and other private parties. There were four demonstration parties, and each party consisting of a supervisor and five *mistries*.[41]

## Mat Weaving Industry

Mats were needed in every home in Orissa and there was great scope for establishing mat weaving as a cottage industry. Mats were made out of reeds, grass, jute, and coconut coir, all of which were available in plenty in Orissa. Most of the mat industries were working at places like Pipili, Sakhigopal, and Chandanpur in Puri district. These industries manufactured different types of finished goods out of coconut coir and other raw materials. After catering to the local needs, they were sent to outside markets. The particular types of mat known as "*sopa*" were greatly in demand. *Sopas* were made in some villages in North Balasore, mostly confined to the Bhogarai police station, where the aquatic plants used in marketing mats grew in abundance. Most of the mats were sent to the other parts of Orissa and Bengal by rail, road and river communication. Mats made with seasonal white reeds were more lasting and fetched better price than those made with fresh reed. Most of the mat weavers were poor, landless labourers and petty cultivators.[42]

## Fishery

Fishery constituted one of the basic food industries in Orissa. It played a vital role in the economic development of the coastal districts of Orissa like Puri, Balasore and Cuttack. Chillika was the most important lake for the rearing of fish. The Chillika Lake covers an area of about 906 sq. km in summer and 1,165 sq. km in rainy seasons. It formed a valuable and compact fishing area for many varieties of tasty fish like mullets, vekti and prawns. Formerly prawns were caught in abundance, but due to some factors it became very problematic to rear prawns. A particular group of people called "*Nolias*" caught fish from the lake through the *Jaal* (net) and sold them in the nearby market. They also exported fish by the railways and ships to Calcutta and Burma. In 1943-44, 77,289 mounds of fish of which 72,480 mounds came from the Chillika Lake, were exported from Orissa by the rail against 51,883 mounds previous year.[43] But this industry lost its importance due to the absence of fishing-curing yards or a cold storage plant to preserve their catch. The fishermen were at the mercy of the exploiting merchants who dictated the price to be paid for the catch.[44]

## Brass and Bell-metal Industry

The brass and bell metal utensils and ornamentals were the most important industries in Orissa. They took a new shape during the early decades of the 20th century with the formation of *Utkal Samilani* (Utkal Union Conference). For the development of this industry, a resolution was made by the delegates at the Sammilani in the year 1904. In this Sammilani, the provision was made for the development and rejuvenation of certain cottage industries, including brass and bell metal industry.[45]

The brass and bell metal products were manufactured in village industries. The brass and bell metal utensils were in common use by the people of Orissa. From that metal, the household utensils and pots, temple accessories, ornaments and decorative wares and curios were made.[46] A large number of workers were engaged in bell metal industries at different places in the province. The famous bell metal producing places were Balakati, Kontiol, Khaliasahi, Bhainchua, Mukatpur in Purí district; Ghontimunda and Bharatpur in Cuttack, and Remuna in Balasore district. The proportion of the different metals in the alloy used for making the articles at different places varied and the articles also varied in quality. Although it was not so much the colour of the metals but the design and workmanship for which the articles made at some places were famous. Some of these articles or utensils used to find a good market outside.[47] The industry had to face stiff competition due to scarcity of the non-ferrous metal in the market, and the consequent rise in prices. Yet it has not declined due to the conventional association of brass and bell metal with the social and cultural life of the people of the country.[48]

**Rice Mill**

Since long Orissa was famous for its rice cultivation. Rice was a major food for all the Oriyas. So paddy cultivation occupied a major portion in the province.

Orissa produced huge amount of paddy and to process the paddy, rice mills were required. So many rice mills came into being in Orissa during the early decades of the 20th century. They employed many people for the processing purpose. It was a seasonal industry. There were as many as 73 rice mills in Orissa, out of these, near about 10 small and big rice mills were situated in Cuttack district.[49] Some of the rice mills were also situated in Puri and Balasore. These mills produced very fine quality of rice like "*Basmati*", most demanding rice in Orissa. It also got its reputation not only in Orissa and other provinces of India, but also abroad. After catering to the demand in the local market in Orissa, the rice was exported from the local ports of Puri, Balaswar and Cuttack for shipping to Calcutta, Mauritius, and Ceylon. It lost its prominance when the merchants from other provinces came to Orissa and started selling machine-produced fine finished rice in the province at a cheaper price.[50]

**Tile Industry**

Tile making was one of the most important industries in Orissa. It was encouraged on a large scale for roofing purpose, so that the straw used for thatching could be released for cattle fodder. In the early twentieth century, a tile factory was established at Nuabazar near Cuttack. This factory started manufacturing tiles for the roofing purpose. It also provided tiles for local market. But this factory lost its reputation due to the manufacture of poor quality tiles which soaked water during the rains, and the availability of good quality Mangalore tiles and Ranigunj tiles in Orissa at cheaper prices. Although most of the employees of the factory went to Bengal to learn tile making, but they could not make good quality tiles.[51]

### Shree Durga Glass Work Pvt. Ltd., Baranga

Shree Durga Glass Works Private Limited was established in the year 1936 by a Marwari industrialist. It was situated at Baranga near the railway station on the Bengal-Nagpur railway, next to Cuttack towards the south.[52] It was the only glass factory in the province of Orissa. It produced items such as glass tumblers, chimneys, lantern globes, bottle, jars, jugs, drinking glasses, paper weights and inkpots, which were used by various local bodies in the province.[53] The factory got almost all its raw materials from outside. It got its requirements of sand from Allahabad and lime from Katni. It used a certain quantity of quartz and sand stone available at Kalapathara and fireclay at Jagannath Prasad which was not far from Baranga. Besides that, a few of the raw materials were also imported from abroad.[54] On 15 June 1937, R.K. Nehru, an ICS officer, deputy secretary, law and commerce, Government of India, directed the provincial governments and local administration for giving assistance to India's certain minor industries to meet Japanese competition, and in Orissa, only Shree Glasswork gave answer to the questions and got assistance from the department of commerce.[55]

### Wool and Silk Industry

The production of wool depended on the number of sheep available. It was not small in Orissa. The cattle census of 1930 shows the figure of sheep as follows:

| | |
|---|---:|
| District of Cuttack | 69,942 |
| District of Puri | 37,867 |
| District of Balasore | 7,358 |
| Total | 115,167 |

There were a large number of sheep in this region. No doubt, the wool of the local sheep was inferior in quality. Still it had some value according to its quality. Long time ago, some families came from Bihar and settled in the town of Cuttack at *Godisahi* and some other places on the other side of the river. They used to keep some of the sheep of better breed brought from their own native places and used to weave *'Assans' a*nd blankets with their wool. Probably they gave up the profession as it did not pay. The experiment was made in the 'poor industry cottage' and was found that the local wool was quite suitable for rough blankets, *assans* and beautiful *galichas*. Some specimens are still preserved in the showroom of the poor industry cottage at Cuttack. Though the experiment was successful, no attempts were made to introduce the industry in the province, on the lines of experiments made. Some years after, another attempt was made by the government to develop the industry by imparting some foreign sheep. Some Bikaner sheep were purchased and distributing to some villagers and other respectable persons with a view to improve breed of the animals and their wool. The attempt proved a failure as the government did not render sufficient guidance beyond disturbing a few Bikanir sheep among the villagers. It need hardly be stated that the villagers were quite ignorant about techniques of the industry. Lastly, for war supply, blanket weaving was introduced by the government with imported wool yarn. Some blankets were woven and supplied. Some people were persuaded for the weaving looms and accessories. They were supplied with wool yarn imported from other provinces, and helped with expert advice to weave the blankets. A number of persons picked off the art of wool weaving. They expected permanent supply of wool yarn.

But it was stopped. Those who practised weaving of wool could not get any advantage of weaving. Those who purchased loom as accessories felt disappointed. The silk was not known in Orissa before 1926. From 1926, the industrial development of Bihar and Orissa started, and the government took some major steps to popularise it. Mulberry silk was used for production of silk cloth at certain places in the districts of Puri and Balasore. Attempt was made from 1928 by the industry department to develop the industry. Some money was spent for rearing of mulberry silk at the agricultural farm at Cuttack. The result of this attempt was not satisfactory and it was stopped.[56]

## Creation of the Department of Industry

Before the creation of the province of Orissa, the Department of Industries in Orissa was the concern of the Department of Industries of the Government of Bihar and Orissa. On the creation of the new province of Orissa, the Department of Industries was placed under the charge of the Director of Development and Industries headed by the Department of Commerce and Industries. The department had five main branches viz, Textile, Technical Education, State Assistance, Fisheries and Labour. For the purpose of advising the director on matters relating to technical education and the working of the department, a board of industries for Orissa was constituted in February in 1939.[57]

## Development of Industrial Schools and Institutions

For the development of industry in Orissa, there were some industrial schools. In 1905, there were three industrial schools in Balasore district, out of these two were aided and one unaided, attended by 116 pupils.

Weaving, carpentry, and blacksmithery were taught in them. The Alalpur Industrial School in Balasore district was the only institution of industrial training. Its founder was an Oriya gentleman, who had raised the standard of craftsmanship in his neighbourhood. In the development of cottage industries in Orissa, the Balasore School played a very vital role. It was managed by the American Christian Mission. This school also trained the boys in metal work and motor repairing. It ranked second among the technical institutions of Orissa, being next to the Orissa School of Engineering.[58]

Further as the technical education developed in Orissa, in 1907 the Government of India gave permission to establish two weaving schools in Orissa. Accordingly, the Sambalpur Weaving School was established in 1911. The control of the schools was transferred from the Director of Public Instruction to the Registrar of Co-operative Societies in September 1915. The subjects taught in these schools included practical weaving, freehand drawing, design, fabric structure, dyeing preparation of yarn and yarn calculation. In 1913, a scheme was introduced by which the government supplied the students with yarn and sale proceeds of the cloth woven by them were credited to government. The profits were used for the purchase of books to be given to those who had completed their courses. However, the scheme proved a failure. On the recommendation of the Registrar, government sanctioned to revert to the old rules under which the weavers provided their own yarn and sold white clothes they made. The school taught about the fancy weaving clothes. The management of the school rested with a local committee. The committee in Sambalpur was presided over by the Deputy Commissioner.[59] The

Cuttack committee was presided over by the District Magistrate of Cuttack.

During the period 1912-17, near about 224 students completed their courses from these schools and 181 books had been distributed to the students. In 1920, the industrial section of the Mission Girl's School was opened at Cuttack. In this school, training was given to girls in basket making, weaving, spinning, sewing and embroidery. In 1930, it was reported to have made satisfactory progress. But the number of students in the shelter industrial school began to decline gradually. During the 1930's, a number of industrial schools were established in every nook and corner of Orissa to provide technical education and hence to eradicate poverty and unemployment in Orissa. These schools used to give instructions in certain useful crafts like weaving, tailoring, toy making, basket making, wood and metal work and so on. These technical institutions were the Madhusudan Village Institution at Cuttack, the Poor Cottage Industry at Cuttack, Basanta Kumari Bidhaba Ashram at Puri, Phulbani Industrial School, Angul Weaving School, Weaving School under the Salvation Army at Angul, and Kujang Industrial School.[60]

Except the Phulbani Industrial School and the Angul Weaving School, all the industrial schools of Orissa were private institutions which received grants-in-aid from the department. In 1936, the number of pupils on the rolls of these schools was 160 and the expenditure met from Government funds was Rs. 16,581.

Rai Bahudur B.C. Patnaik was the founder of the Orissa Poor Cottage Industries. Its chief aim was training students in different handicrafts by using raw materials available locally. It had different sections like weaving basket, can and mat, toy, tailoring, women section, etc. The number of students in this institution was 25 in 1936. Another industrial school, namely, Basanta Kumari Bidhaba Ashram, was meant solely for women. It was managed by Soraj Nalini Association of Calcutta and was primarily a boarding school for training them in handicrafts.[61] In 1936-37, a new industrial institution, called, Madhusudan Village Industries Institution, was started at Cuttack, by a private association with the financial aid of Rs. 23,620 from the government, which undertook to maintain it for the first five years. The school had eight sections like weaving of khaddar, silk and woolen cloths and durris, cane work, soap making, paper making, oil pressing, manufacture of phenyile, ink, toy making, dyeing and printing.[62]

In 1942-43, the following private institutions received grant-in-aid from the government[63]:

| |  |  |
|---|---|---|
| 1. | The Balasore Technical School | Rs. 5,400 |
| 2. | The Shelter Industrial School, Cuttack | Rs. 1,200 |
| 3. | The Orissa Poor Cottage Industry, Cuttack | Rs. 1,000 |
| 4. | The Basanta Kumari Bidhaba Ashram, Puri | Rs. 780 |
| 5. | The Weaving School under Angul Central Co-operative Banking Union Ltd. | Rs. 120 |
| 6. | The Weaving School under Salvation Army | Rs. 1,008 |
| 7. | The Madhusudan Village Industries Institution, Cuttack | Rs. 15,000 |
| | Total | Rs. 24, 508 |

Besides these industrial schools, there were craft schools opened with a view to enabling the villagers to pursue useful vocations during the off seasons. The crafts schools aimed at imparting training in such subjects as jute weaving, basket making, cane work, bamboo work, etc., for which raw materials were available in the villages.

**Industrial Working Class in Colonial Orissa**

The province of Orissa was mainly an agricultural region and most of its people lived in villages. In the caste-based rural society, a particular craft was practised by a particular caste hereditarily. The weavers produced clothes, carpenters worked in wood, blacksmiths engaged themselves in gold and silver, potters took up pottery works. The village weavers used to manufacture their products through *Tantas* (handmade looms). The weavers were identified in the society as *tantis*. With the help of these primitive instruments, it was not possible on the part of the weavers to get good outturns to compete with the mill made textiles in the markets of Orissa.[64]

Although the people's chief occupation in the plain was agriculture, but the people living very close to the sea and the river, earned their livelihood by making salt and catching fish. Many were also dependent on handicrafts, weaving and wood cutting, but in the jungle tracts, there were of course cultivating classes clinging to their hereditary field. In certain areas, they burnt down patches of forest or scrubs and the part of land on which they grew paddy and cotton. But the aboriginal tribes in general constituted a class of landless day labourers.

In Orissa, we can find three types of labourers. The first was agriculture labour, those who depended on an agricultural field throughout the year. The second was seasonal labour; those who depended on the agricultural field as well as on cottage industries. The last was semi-skilled labour and skilled labour; these constituted a small group of population and were totally dependent upon the traditional industries in Orissa. The first two constituted of major portion of the population.

**Employment of Industrial Labour**

Orissa was not developed industrially before or during the colonial period. One of the most peculiar thing is that, during the early decade of the twentieth century when Orissa's most neighbouring provinces like Bihar and Bengal were industrially developed, comparatively at that time Orissa was one of the industrially backward provinces in the whole of India, particularly in the Bengal Presidency, in spite of abundant availability of raw materials and unskilled labour. Although at that time in Orissa, there was no industry, there were however many cottage industries there. For the manufacturing goods many people were employed in those cottage industries.

The gold and silver work was the most important industry in Cuttack district. These industries gave employment to about 400 families in the interiors. These labourers were both skilled as well as unskilled. They earned their livelihood by selling these articles in the nearer as well as foreign market. They worked there to create articles by mixing gold with an ally of silver and copper and of silver alloyed with copper.[65] These filigree workers were trained in the School of Art Wares. Another important industry was silk weaving. In these industries, the labourers were migrated to Cuttack from Burdwan or Midinapore. There were about 600 persons engaged in the industry, who were the descendants of the weavers who settled in Cuttack about seven generations. Almost every family had their an own loom.

They earned money from them and managed to earn about 2 *annas* a day per person without having to take to any subsidiary profession. The mat weaving industries provided employment to hundreds of workers, both men and women. Likewise, the cane work industries of Cuttack provided employment to a number of skilled labourers; they were trained from Madhusudan Village Industries Institute and Poor Cottage Industries.[66] In the coir industries, 30 villages, more than 521 families, constituting a population of 2344 of the Sadar Subdivision of Puri district were engaged. They used to make rope by using coconut coir. The artisans were sufficiently skilled in the art of rope-making but had a very low income from their trade.[67] There were about 3,000 (300 families) carpenters engaged in the district of Cuttack alone in wood working and furniture. Here the profession had been taken up by those of other castes than the hereditary carpenters. Besides carpentry work, they were also engaged in agricultural activities.[68] Another important private industry which gave maximum employment in Orissa was Shree Durga Glass Work. For manufacturing goods, it had given employment to 639 persons, both skilled and semi-skilled.[69] But one thing was that they were not trained properly for the glass work. That is why, this industry did not manufacture good quality glass products.[70] In 1939, a major industrial unit, Oriental Paper Mills, came up in Brajarajnager with nearly 4,500 workers working in it. The coal mining industry of Orissa and Bengal made some progress owing to the growth of factories and extension of railway and steamship.[71] Keeping the above-mentioned purpose in mind, in Orissa, the Raja of Talcher (a princely state) leased out 3 coalfields to European companies in 1921. In these coal mines many of the unskilled labourers from

Talcher as well as the adjacent areas worked.[72] The construction of railways further accelerated the employment of labour in most part of Orissa. The construction of the Bengal-Nagpur Railway Company, Balasore Railway Committee and the expansion of railway lines to the interior *Gadajat* (princely state) areas provided work to both *bethi* (unpaid) and wage labourers.[73] Simultaneously, the construction of Tata Iron and Steel Company was started in 1908 at a village called Sakchi, which later became the steel city of Jamshedpur, and the Maharaja of Mayurbhanj, Sri Ramachandra Bhanja, granted three iron mines at Gorumahishani, Badampahar and Sulaipahar of Mayurbhanj, in which many unskilled and *bethi* (unpaid) labourers worked.[74]

According to the statistics obtained at the census of 1901, in Puri district, 60 per cent of the populations were supported by agriculture, 16.5 per cent by industries, 0.4 per cent by commerce and four per cent by profession. Of the industrial population, 53 per cent were actual workers among whom were 10,000 fishermen and fish dealers, 5,000 cow-keepers, milk-sellers, etc., 12,000 grain preachers, 6,000 rice-pounders, 11,000 sellers of firewood and charcoal, 9,000 cotton weavers and spinners, 5,000 basket-weavers and mat-makers, as well as numerous goldsmiths, braziers, coppersmiths, potters and carpenters.[75]

So far as industrial labour is concerned, in Puri district, 114,360 or 12 per cent were engaged in industry. Out of these, 17,699 were engaged in textiles (including 11,100 weavers and 4,300 rope makers); 12,556 were workers in wood and basketwork; 7,641 were metal workers; 7,403 were workers in lac, glass, etc. 28,826 were engaged in the preparation of food, rice pounding and so on; 26,968 were makers of dress, tailors, etc. And the rest were in miscellaneous trades such as building, bangle making, etc. Only nine per cent or 80,759 people were engaged in trade.[76]

The report of the inspector of factories for the year 1929 showed ten factories within the meaning of the Indian Factory Act. These consist of two government factories, namely, the Public Works Department Workshop at Jobar, in which the iron and woodwork required for the maintenance of the anicut, locks and canals was turned out and the workshop attached to the Orissa School of Engineering, two printing presses, one railway workshop, one rice mill, two dal mills, one match factory and one tannery. The total number of hands employed was only 586 of whom 376 were employed in the two government workshops.[77]

According to the annual report of the Department of Industries for 1947, there were 184 industries working in Orissa, as against 122 in 1946. The total daily average number of labour employed in all the 184 industries were 10,592, against 7,443 industries of the previous year. Out of 184 industries in Orissa in 1947, 83 industries were working in the three coastal districts of Cuttack, Puri, and Balasore. Out of 86 industries in Cuttack district, 37 industries were working during the reported time as against 21 in the previous year. In these 37 industries, 2,115 labourers were employed as against 1,520 in the previous year. The increase was mainly due to the establishment of one textile rolling mill, in addition to some Bidi factories, which were registered during the year. In the Balasore district, numbers of industries worked during the year under the report were 34 as against 32 in the previous year. The average numbers of labour employed were 1,944 against 1,602 in the previous year. This was due to the establishment of one new oil mill and one new rice mill in the district. The total number of industries worked in Puri district, rose from six to nine during the year under report and daily average number of labour employed were 727.[78]

One of the most important industries during the early decades of the twentieth century in Orissa was handloom weaving industries. These industries provided employment to a numbers of weavers, among them most were trained from the different industrial schools in Orissa. They formed many weaving parties and co-operatives in order to protect themselves. These industries took practical shape with the formation of Orissa as a separate province and the establishment of the Department of Development of which industrial department became a part.[79]

**The Wages of Labourers**

As far as labourers' wages are concerned, there were no fixed wages for the labourers in colonial Orissa. It was because most of the industries were not organised, most of labourers were not skilled and were not organised. That's why, their wages varied from work to work, industry to industry, and place to place. Here we present an analysis of the wages of the industrial labourers of three coastal districts (Cuttack, Puri, and Balasore) of Orissa. In the Puri district, the wages commonly paid for skilled labour were low. Masons were paid six to eight annas per person according to skill; carpenters and blacksmiths were paid five to eight annas. While in the towns male coolies got four annas and female coolies and boys got two annas as their daily wage.[80] Further in the district of Puri, the wages for skilled labour varied from Rs. 0-6-0 to Rs. 1-3-9 as against Rs. 0-2-0 to Rs. 0-6-0 for unskilled labour. In the Cuttack district, the daily wages for skilled labour varied from

Rs. 0-5-0 to Rs. 1-6-0 as against Rs. 2-6-0 to Rs. 0-6-0 for unskilled labour. In the Balasore district, the daily wages for skilled labour varied from Rs. 0-5-9 to Rs. 1-2-0 as against Rs. 0-4-0 to Rs. 0-6-6 for unskilled labour.[81]

According to the annual report of the year, 1937-38, in the Cuttack district the unskilled labourers were getting Rs. three to Rs. seven. Whereas the skilled labourers got Rs. seven in Puri district, the wages of unskilled labourers were about the same as for agricultural labour. They varied from Rs. two to Rs. three in the rural areas and from Rs. four to Rs. six in the urban areas. And the skilled labourer was paid monthly. In the Balasore district, there were the wages of agricultural and industrial labour. All the unskilled labour in this district came from the aboriginal element of the neighbouring feudatory states.[82]

**Statistics of the Labour Wages in Cuttack**

| *Years* | | *1910* | | | *1920* | | | *1930* | |
|---|---|---|---|---|---|---|---|---|---|
| *Artisans* | *Rs.* | *a.* | *p.* | *Rs.* | *a.* | *p.* | *Rs.* | *a* | *p.* |
| Blacksmith | 0 | 8 | 0 | 0 | 10 | 0 | 0 | 12 | 0 |
| | | to | | | to | | | to | |
| | 1 | 0 | 0 | 1 | 2 | 0 | 1 | 4 | 0 |
| Mason | 0 | 8 | 0 | 0 | 10 | 0 | 0 | 12 | 0 |
| | | to | | | to | | | to | 0 |
| | 0 | 12 | 0 | 1 | 0 | 0 | 1 | 4 | |
| Carpenter | 0 | 8 | 0 | 0 | 10 | 0 | 0 | 12 | 0 |
| | | to | | | to | | | to | 0 |
| | 0 | 12 | 0 | 1 | 0 | 0 | 1 | 4 | |
| Gharami | 0 | 3 | 6 | 0 | 4 | 0 | 0 | 5 | 0 |
| | | to | | | to | | | to | 0 |
| | 0 | 4 | 0 | 0 | 6 | 0 | 0 | 8 | |
| Unskilled labourer | 0 | 3 | 0 | 0 | 4 | 0 | 0 | 5 | 0 |
| Ploughman | 0 | 3 | 0 | 0 | 4 | 0 | 0 | 4 | 0 |

*Sources:* L.S.S. O' Malley, Bihar and Orissa District Gazetteers, Cuttack, 1933, p. 142.

**District Wise Workers and Wages for Different Categories (1941-42 to 1942-43)**

| *Name of the District* | *Number of Labourers Employed in Factory* | *Wages for Skilled Labour* | | *Wages for Unskilled Labour* | | *Wages of Agricultural Labour* | |
|---|---|---|---|---|---|---|---|
| | | *1941-42* | *1942-43* | *1941-42* | *1942-43* | *1941-42* | *1942-43* |
| 1 | 2 | 3 | 4 | 5 | 6 | 7 | 8 |
| | | Rs. a. p. | Rs. a. p. | Rs. a. p. | Rs. a. p. | Rs. a. p. | Rs. a. p. |
| Cuttack | 2,127 | 0 5 0 to 1 6 0 | 0 6 0 to 1 6 0 | 0 2 6 to 0 6 0 | 0 3 0 to 0 8 0 | 0 2 0 to 0 5 0 | 0 3 0 to 0 8 0 |
| Balasore | 1,824 | 0 5 9 to 1 2 0 | 0 6 0 to 1 3 0 | 0 4 0 to 0 6 0 | 0 4 0 to 0 6 0 | 0 4 0 to 0 6 0 | 0 4 0 to 0 6 0 |
| Puri | 435 | 0 6 0 to 1 3 9 | 0 6 0 to 1 3 0 | 0 2 0 to 0 6 0 | 0 4 0 to 1 2 0 | 0 2 0 to 0 4 0 | 0 3 0 to 0 6 0 |

*Sources:* Annual Report for the year 1943-44, Department of Industry, Orissa, page No. 10.

**District Wise Workers and Wages for Different Categories (1943-44 to 1944-45)**

| *Name of the District* | *Number of Labourers Employed in Factory* | | *Wages for Skilled Labour* | | *Wages for Unskilled Labour* | | *Wages of Agricultural Labour* | |
|---|---|---|---|---|---|---|---|---|
| | *1943-1944* | *1944-1945* | *1943-44* | *1944-45* | *1943-44* | *1944-45* | *1943-44* | *1944-45* |
| *1* | *2* | *3* | *4* | *5* | *6* | *7* | *8* | *9* |
| | | | Rs. a. p. | Rs. a. p. | Rs. a. p. | Rs. a. p. | Rs. a. p. | Rs. a. p. |
| Cuttack | 1,970 | 1,865 | 0 10 0 to 2 0 0 | 0 10 0 to 2 0 0 | 0 3 0 to 0 8 0 | 0 6 0 to 0 9 0 | 0 5 0 to 0 12 0 | 0 5 0 to 1 0 0 |
| Balasore | 1,615 | 1,142 | 0 6 0 to 1 5 0 | 0 12 0 to 1 8 0 | 0 4 0 to 0 7 0 | 0 5 0 to 0 6 0 | 0 8 0 to 0 12 0 | 0 5 0 to 0 10 0 |
| Puri | 467 | 539 | 0 7 0 to 0 1 5 | 1 4 0 to 1 8 0 | 0 8 0 to 0 12 0 | 0 12 0 to 1 0 0 | 0 5 0 to 0 8 0 | 0 6 0 to 0 8 0 |

*Sources:* Annual Report for the year 1944-45, Department of Industry, Orissa, p. 12.

**District Wise Maximum and minimum Wages for Different Skilled/Unskilled (1946-47 to 1947-48)**

| *District* | *Maximum* | | *Minimum* | |
|---|---|---|---|---|
| | *1946-47* | *1947-48* | *1946-47* | *1947-48* |
| | *Rs. a p* | *Rs. a p* | *Rs. a p* | *Rs. a p* |
| **Cuttack** | | | | |
| Skilled | 1 8 0 | 2 8 0 | 0 13 0 | 1 8 0 |
| Unskilled | 0 12 3 | 0 14 3 | 0 6 0 | 0 12 0 |
| **Balasore** | | | | |
| Skilled | 2 0 0 | 2 0 0 | 0 9 6 | 1 8 0 |
| Unskilled | 0 10 0 | 1 0 0 | 0 6 0 | 0 12 0 |
| **Puri** | | | | |
| Skilled | 2 14 0 | 3 0 0 | 0 14 0 | 0 8 0 |
| Unskilled | 0 11 9 | 1 0 0 | 0 8 4 | 0 12 0 |

*Sources:* Annual Report for the year 1947-48, Department of Industry, Orissa, p. 23.

The above tables shows the movement of wages for the principal classes of labourers for the first three decades of the twentieth century. The tables show that there was very little increase in the wages of labourers from 1910 to 1930. They only demonstrates the continued exploitation of the labourers in colonial Orissa. Besides these, sawyers, stone-cutters, bricklayers, and tailors got Rs. four.

*Statistics of the wages of labour in three coastal districts (Cuttack, Balasore, Puri), of Orissa, from 1941 to 1947.*

**The Conditions and Welfare of Labourers**

As far as Orissa is concerned, it was part of Bengal Presidency and had not tasted the fruits of industrialisation. So, most of the Orissa's labour had gone to other parts of India for seeking employment. But in Orissa, at the same time, some cottage and small scale industries were there. Many labourers were working in those industries. For them, no specific rules and regulations were there till the formation of Trade Union Congress in 1935 and Industrial Disputes Act of 1945. But in order to ventilate their grievances and for the welfare of the labour, some co-operatives were there, like Weaving Co-operative Societies and so on.

Labour welfare, in a wider term, means everything that contributes to the improvement of health, safety, general well-being of the workers. In Orissa, the labourers were mainly classified under two categories i, e., agriculture labourers and industrial labourers. The major portion of the total work force of the three districts was agricultural labourers. The agriculture labourers had no organisation like trade union to ventilate their grievances before their employers. They were not covered under any social security scheme to take care of unemployment, accidents and other hazards.

Industrially the district was not advanced. However, there were industrial estates at Jagatpur and Khapuria. There were some major and minor plants like textiles mills, spinning, rice mills, flour mills, saw mills, printing press, bidi factories, and so on. So, the workers of these industries formed so many organisations by individuals, companies, corporations, and co-operative societies. A number of them also worked in different commercial establishments. These workers protected their interests through their trade unions and associations, etc. The workers in rural areas were deprived of such type of benefits.[83] In Cuttack district, they formed Press Workers Union, Shree Durgadas Workers Union, Tailoring Workers Union, Commercial Workers Union, and so on. In Puri district, they formed Puri Electric Workers Union; and in Balasore, they formed Balasore Zilla Rice Mills Union and so on.

In Sambalpur, Oriental Paper Mills was one important industry there. The workers of that industry formed Oriental Paper Mills Association through which they ventilated their grievances before the management of the mill. In January 1941, the workers of Oriental Paper Mills went on strike and threatened the manager of the mill on the question of bonus. So, out of pressure the manager of the mill agreed on 10 January to pay gratuity of 15 days to all workers, who had completed a minimum service of six months in the factory.[84] In May 1943, 200 workers of IB River Colliery of Sambalpur went on strike, demanding enhancement of wages. The workers resumed their work on 18th May 1943, after the authority promised to pay an increment of *four Anna* (25 paisa) per worker and coolies from July of the same month.[85] Trade unions were voluntary associations of employees formed under the Trade Union Act to promote and protect their interests through collective actions and securing them a better and healthier status in industry as well as in the society.[86] For the welfare of labourers, the owner of the industry had to provide bonus and some sanitation facilities, housing and water supply, which however was very much wanting in colonial Orissa.

## Conclusion

During the nineteenth century, Orissa was not developed industrially because of lack of interest on the part of those who had capital with them and due to the various hindrances. But the process of industrialisation took new shape during the last decade of nineteenth century and early decade of twentieth century with the introduction of railway lines as a means of communication, growth of technical education and emergence of capitalists on the soil of Orissa. For the development of cottage and small scale industries, the credit goes to Madhusudan Das, the maker of modern Orissa. He first injected the idea of Swadeshi in the mind and the soul of millions of Orissa's people well before the starting of the Swadeshi movement in Bengal with introducing Orissa Art Wares, the first organised industry in Orissa at Cuttack in the year 1899-1900. It was followed by the installation of Utkal Tannery, a world famous shoe factory, at Cuttack in 1905. The filigree work (work on thin and silver ware) of Cuttack got high reputation not only in Cuttack and Orissa but also in most of the European and South Asian countries of the world. The organised sector industrial labour started in the early years of the first decade of the twentieth century, when Madhusudan Das set up an organised industry, Orissa Art Wares and then Utkal Tannery Shoe Factory. The beginning of the organised skilled labour goes back to early years of twentieth century, when Orissa Arts Ware employed 100 men initially for the high quality of production and a separate school of Arts Ware was attached to the factory. Further the wages of the industrial labourers were varied from person to person and place to place, probably the skilled labour got high wages than the unskilled labours. Through the unions and co-operatives, the labourers ventilated their grievances and through the negotiation, arbitration they were able to somehow increase their salaries and so on. In brief, the emergence of industry and the formation of working class were remarkable phenomena in the annals of socio-economic life of the people of Orissa in the first half of the twentieth century. It opened a new chapter in the history of colonial Orissa.

## References

1. A.K. Bagchi, *Private Investment in India (1900-1936)*, New Delhi, 1972, p. 1.
2. Bipan Chandra, The *Rise and Growth of Economic Nationalism* (1880- 1905), New Delhi, 1966, p. 55.
3. H.B. Mohanty, *An Industrial Survey of Orissa*, Cuttack, 1945, p. 1.
4. J.K. Samal, *Economic History of Orissa (1866-1947)*, New Delhi, 2000, p. 100.
5. P.C. Das, *The Economic History of Orissa in the 19th Century*, New Delhi, 1989, p. 223.
6. J.K. Samal, *op. cit.*, p. 101.
7. P.C. Das, *op. cit.*, pp. 241-42.
8. Orissa State Archive (OSA) (ed.), *Madhubabu and Orissa in Making*, Bhubaneswar,1999, p. 152.
9. J.K. Samal , *op.cit.*, p. 69.

10. S.N. Mohanty, *Madhusudan Das*, Cuttack, 1972, pp. 71-72.
11. OSA, *op.cit.*, p. 160.
12. *Ibid.*, p. 155.
13. S.N. Mohanty, *op.cit.*, p. 136.
14. Utkal Dipika, 14th January, 1911 (OSA).
15. OSA, *op. cit.*, p. 153.
16. S.C. Bhola, *British Economic Policy in Orissa*, New Delhi, 1990, p. 113.
17. *Utkal Dipika*, 24th November, 1906, (OSA).
18. S.N. Mohanty, *op.cit.*, p. 115.
19. *Utkal Dipika*, 1908, p. 547 (NMM&L), New Delhi.
20. OSA, *op. cit.*, pp. 163-164.
21. *Ibid.*, p. 41.
22. S.C. Bhola, *op. cit.*, p. 113.
23. H.B. Mohanty, *op. cit.*, p. 6.
24. D.K. Das, *Utkal Sammilani (1903-1936)*, Rourkela, 2005, pp. 191-193.
25. S.S.O. Malley, *Bihar and Orissa District Gazetteer, Cuttack*, Patna, 1933, p. 150.
26. H.B. Mohanty, *op.cit.*, p. 61.
27. *Ibid.*, p. 61.
28. *Report on the survey of Cottage and Small Scale Industry in the Districts of Orissa, 1960*, p. 27 (OSA).
29. N.C. Behuria, (ed.), *Orissa District Gazetteers, Cuttack*, govt. of Orissa, 1992, p. 350.
30. H.B. Mohanty, *op.cit.*, p. 52.
31. Report, (Small Scale Industry), *op. cit.*, p. 29 (OSA).
32. N. Senapati, (ed), *Orissa District Gazetteers, Puri*, Govt. of Orissa, 1977, p. 234.
33. H.B. Mohanty, *op. cit*, pp. 51-52.
34. H.B. Mohanty, *op.cit*, p. 51.

35. *Ibid.*, pp. 49-50.
36. File No. 19- 139/37, *Education Department (industry)*, Govt. of Orissa, Sept. 1937 (OSA).
37. File No. 19/37, *Department Industry and Labour*, Govt. of India, No. 1354 (OSA).
38. Annual Report, 1936-37, *Department of Development (Industry)* Orissa, p. 5 (OSA).
39. *Ibid.*, p. 6.
40. *Annual Report, 1937-38, Industry*, pp. 8-9 (OSA).
41. *Annual Report, 1939-40, Industry*, pp. 40-41 (OSA).
42. *Ibid.*, pp. 29-31 (OSA).
43. Annual report, 1943-44, Industry, Chapter- VIII, pp. 12 (OSA).
44. H.B. Mohanty, *op. cit*, p. 57.
45. D.K. Das, *op. cit*, p.110.
46. N. Mohapatra (Puri), *op. cit*, p. 237.
47. H.B. Mohanty, *op. cit*, p. 53.
48. N. Mohapatra (Puri), *op. cit*, p. 237.
49. H.B. Mohanty, *op.cit*, p. 57.
50. L.S.S.O, Malley, (Cuttack), 1933, p. 158.
51. H.B. Mohanty, *op. cit*, p. 37.
52. N.C. Behuria, (ed.) Cuttack, *op. cit*, p. 3.
53. File No. III, 9-29/38, *Education Department, (Industry)*, Govt. of Orissa, 1938, p. 5 (OSA).
54. H.B. Mohanty, *op.cit.*, p. 33.
55. File No. 19-119/87, *Education Department, (Industry)*, Govt. of Orissa, Sept. 1937 (OSA).
56. S.C. Bhola, *op. cit.*, pp. 111-12.
57. *Annual report, 1936-37, Industry*, p. 1 (OSA).
58. J.K. Samal, *History of Education in Orissa (1905-1936)*, Calcutta, 1984, pp. 110-12.
59. *Ibid.*, p. 135.

60. *Report on the progress on Education in Orissa, 1936-37*, Govt. of Orissa, pp. 75-79 (OSA).
61. *Report, 1942-47, Industry, Chapter VII* (OSA).
62. *Annual Report, 1943-44, Industry*, p. 8 (OSA).
63. *Annual Report, 1942-43, Industry, Chapter-I* (OSA).
64. P.C. Das, *The Economic History of the Orissa in the 19th Century*, New Delhi, 1989, p. 223.
65. L.S.S. Malley, *Bihar and Orissa District Gazetteers*, Cuttack, Patna, 1933, p. 150.
66. H.B. Mohanty, *op. cit*, p. 62.
67. *Report of the Survey of Industries, 1960*, pp. 28-29 (OSA).
68. S.C. Bhola, *op. cit.*, p. 104.
69. N.C. Behuria, (ed.) Cuttack, *op. cit*. p. 104.
70. H.B. Mohanty, *op.cit*, p. 34.
71. D. Basu, *The Working Class in Bengal*, Calcutta,1993, p. 333.
72. A.C. Pradhan and A.K. Patnaik, (ed.), *Peoples's Movements in Orissa (During the Colonial Era)*, Bhubaneswar, 1994, p. 179.
73. Ravi, Ahuja, *Pathways of Empire: Circulation, 'Public Works' and Social Space in Colonial Orissa c. 1880-1914*, Hyderabad, p. 280.
74. *Report of the Administration of Mayurbhanj 1905-06 and 1912-13*, (OSA).
75. L.S.S.O., Malley, (Puri), *op. cit*, p. 180.
76. *Ibid.*, p. 201.
77. *Ibid.*, p. 154.
78. *Annual Report, 1947-48, Industry, Chapter- VII* (OSA).
79. *Annual Report, 1936- 37, Industry,* p. 1 (OSA).
80. L.S.S.O., Malley (Puri), *op. cit.*, pp. 174-75.
81. *Annual Report, 1937-38, Industry*, p. 10 (OSA).
82. *Annual Report, 1940-41, Industry,* p. 11 (OSA).

83. N.C. Behuria, (Cuttack), *op. cit*, p. 929.
84. File No. 18/41, *Home-Political (confidential), fortnightly report, District of Sambalpur, 1941*, p. 4 (OSA)
85. File No. 12/43, *Home-political, Sambalpur, 1943*, p. 98. (OSA).
86. N.C. Behuria, (Cuttack), *op. cit*. p. 932.

# 8

# Working Class Resistance in Travancore: A Study of Punnapra Vayalar Struggle of 1946

***Bibin Kuriakose***

The British established their supremacy in Kerala partly through direct conquest and partly through imposed unequal political and trade treaties. The violent colonial incursions were intended to drain the resources of the subjugated territories and to impose colonial culture on the people by disrupting their way of life.[1] Of the three political units on the Malabar Coast, Malabar District, was retained under the Company's direct rule, and Travancore and Cochin States were placed under indirect rule of the British administration. Travancore occupies a prominent position among the Princely States of the then India. The Princely States were characterised as the trusted pillars of British rule in India. Although they did not undergo the trauma of conquest or political subjugation, they were subordinated in all respects to the British administrative control and exploitation of resources and the people. Travancore was pre-eminently an agricultural country and 47.2 per cent of the population depended for their means of livelihood almost exclusively upon land.[2] The penetration of capitalist enterprises resulted in the growth of modern industries in the state of Travancore. Majority of the industries were owned by European capitalists and side by side the indigenous capitalists also started small scale plantations and industries. With the increase of the capitalist class and the factories of modern kind, the working class also began to emerge in the state.

Alleppey and Quilon were the two important port towns and leading manufacturing centers of Travancore. Textiles, coir, coir mattings, ceramics, chemicals, printing, metals and fish processing were the important industries in the State. The worldwide growth of labour consciousness during 1920-1930 had its repercussions in the State of Travancore also. The workers becoming conscious of their disabilities discovered the means of mitigating their conditions and realised that their lot could be bettered by combined struggles. They, therefore, formed into trade unions and collectively bargained for their rights.[3] The first union registered under the Trade Union Act was Travancore Coir Factory Workers Union and this union coordinated and led the entire trade union activities in the State. By this time the national movement and the demand for responsible government in the form of popular rule in these States reached its zenith. The Princely States and their rulers, as pillars and supporters of British Raj, came into conflict with their subjects who wanted to overthrow both the monarchical and colonial orders.

The people's wish to establish popular rule in the State of Travancore had a very early history and it reached its momentum after the formation of the Travancore State Congress in 1938. The highly autocratic Diwan of the State, Sir C.P. Ramaswamy Aiyar, rejected the plea of the people from the outset of his regime and made certain lies against the popular demand for the responsible government in the State, "that the power of a ruler of an Indian State to grant measures of responsible government is restricted by the necessity of obtaining the explicit consent of the paramount power".[4] Contrary to the statement of Sir C.P. Ramaswamy Aiyer, Earl Winterton stated in the House of Commons that "It is not the policy of the paramount power in ordinary circumstances to intervene in the internal administration of full powered State. In particular, I can assure that the paramount power would certainly not obstruct proposals for constitutional advance initiated by a ruler."[5] Despite of this, Diwan of Travancore put all hurdles in the working of the Travancore State Congress and started branding the organisation as a communal body. Rejecting the claims made by the Diwan, the President of the Travancore State Congress, Pattom Thanu Pillai, stated that "the State Congress is a non-communal organisation independent of all communities and the members of the organisation are drawn from all communities."[6] The surging of new and vital waves of national freedom in the British Indian provinces raised new hopes in the minds of Travancoreans and the movement for responsible government gained momentum throughout the State.

But the Travancore State Congress from the incipient stage followed a reluctant attitude towards the working class solidarity on class lines. The State Congress leaders pointed out that "unity of labourers means not engage in political affairs or convening strikes to overthrow the existing government but mainly to capture their economic rights and demands through legitimate methods."[7] The radical State Congress leaders with socialist leanings later turned to be as Communists followed a pro-labour policy and actively assisted in the formation of trade unions. They had decided to bring the grievances of industrial workers and agricultural labourers to the forefront of the national struggle and fight against the inhuman exploitation of the landlords and the newly emerged capitalists in the State.[8]

The formation of Communist Party in 1939 at Pinarayi in Malabar and the formation of the Travancore Communist Party in 1942 gave a new dimension and class orientation to the working class movement in Kerala as a whole and in the State of Travancore, in particular.[9] The social and economic condition of working class was very miserable in the State of Travancore. Workers were subjected to numerous types of inhuman exploitation and injustice by the *jenmies*, industrialists and factory owners. Majority of the workers in Alleppey and Quilon were the tenants of the landlords. One of the main factors which attracted these labourers to newly formed factories was the daily employment and better wages as compared to their caste-based agricultural operations in the countryside. The Great Economic Depression of 1930's and Second World War brought untold miseries to the agricultural population and industrial workers in the State.[10] The people of Travancore mostly depended on coconut for their livelihood and the price of coconut heavily fell in the depression years. The coir yarning industry also suffered a setback during these crucial years. The employers reduced the numbers of labourers and 6-10 per cent wages were cut.[11] During this period, one can see a phenomenal increase in the trade union consciousness among the workers of the State and separate trade unions were organised in agrarian areas as well as in the industrial belts. But the government imposed ban on the trade union activities and arrested the trade union leaders.

The outbreak of the Second World War precipitated the crisis in the State of Travancore, which had already suffered under the economic depression. The main item of export, coir industry, faced a virtual collapsc by the slump of export to the European countries. Unemployment became rampant in the State and it reached the unbearable limits in coir industry.[12] The shortage of food stuffs, followed by black marketing and hoarding, severely affected the working class population. No concrete measures were taken by the government except passing Travancore Essential Commodities Act on 15th December 1941. But these measures attained no considerable changes in the acute shortage of essential commodities.[13]

The trade unions in the State demanded the proper distribution of the essential commodities through fair shops, but no steps were taken by the government in this regard. For the purpose of uniting all the trade unions in the State, a meeting was convened in Alleppey under the presidency of veteran trade union leader, P. Krishnapillai. Two hundred persons, representing various trade unions in the State, attended the conference. The Travancore Trade Union Congress was born out of the meeting and it elected T.V. Thomas of Communist Party and N. Sreekantan Nair of Socialist Party as President and General Secretary of Travancore Trade Union Congress, respectively.[14] Under the eminent leadership of T.V. Thomas, the working class of Travancore secured so many benefits, both material and moral, and also the trade unions transformed into more aggressive character.[15] By the Japanese occupation of Burma, the import of rice and other essential food items to the State had come to a standstill and people suffered badly because of the acute shortage of food items. The Diwan himself admitted it in assembly, "I am now marking to the honourable members of this house and through them outside that tapioca that fish will be the only things on which we live."[16] The acute shortage of food affected heavily the coir factory workers in Shertallai and Amballapuzha areas. The coir sector alone witnessed 2500 workers as unemployed.[17] The immediate result was that a famine took a toll of twenty thousand people at Shertallai (one of the Taluk in Travancore State) alone. In the words of George Karot, the Vicar of Thankipilli Church at Shertallai, "the death rate was intensified three times than from the outbreak of the war and the coastal people especially labours facing a very pitiable stage."[18]

By the entry of Russia into the war, the Communist Party of India decided to take a pro-British attitude and decided to cooperate with war efforts. The Travancore unit of the Communist Party also made clear about their stand towards the new developments in the World War and urged the labourers to involve in constructive work programmes.[19] The labourers, under the banner of Communist Party, actively engaged in 'Grow More Food

Campaign' in the villages. The political decision of Communist Party to support the war activities alienated them from the main stream national movement and freedom struggle of the State for a short period, but 'Grow More Food Campaign' and the constructive work waged by the party and trade unions during the war had given wide acceptability among the common sections of society and it actually strengthened the party at grassroot level. The Diwan of Travancore blamed the Communist Party and its opportunistic stand taken before the entry of Russia into the war and after the entry. Apart from these, he had taken stringent measures to contain Communist influences in the State. "I may assure you that anybody who insists on shouting 'long live revolution' or 'Inquilab Zindabad' will find himself in jail or will be detained in Travancore. Any labour organisation which had alignment with any political party will not have encouragement from the government."[20] At the same time, he went to Delhi and secured several work orders for the coir industry to solve the serious unemployment situation prevailing in the State. But it was not a panacea to the crucial situation which prevailed in the State.

The Second World War came to an end with the long lasting impact on world economy and politics. In the words of N. Sreekantan Nair, General Secretary of All Travancore Trade Union Congress, "Industries were in stagnation since the war order that stimulated them earlier no longer existed now. Employers and factory owners resorted to large scale retrenchment. They imposed wage cuts and small factories closed their shutters. Thousands of working class families were pushed into starvation. Unemployment became rampant with the arrival of the soldiers who had been demobilised at the end of the World War, shortage of essential goods, hoarding and blackmarketing resulted in steep increase in prices. Life became miserable to most of the population and in addition to these the ruling authorities, especially Diwan, followed repressive policy towards the working class and trade unions."[21]

By the end of the war, Diwan announced his intention of reforming the Constitution of Travancore. The constitutional reform proposal with irremovable executive aroused much criticism and against the Westminster or British system of parliamentary government. In the new Constitution, the position of Diwan will be approximated to that of President of U.S.A. subject always to the rights and prerogatives of a sovereign.[22] The State Congress started the agitation against the Constitutional reforms in the initial stage, but in the meanwhile some of its leaders, especially Pattom Thanupillai (President of State Congress), followed a soft corner towards the new Constitution propagated by Diwan. However, the working class under the banner of Communist Party started the struggle against the American model constitutional reforms and raised the slogan American Model Arabi Kadalil, i.e., "American Model in Arabian Sea".[23] Fully antagonist towards working class and Communist Party, the Diwan started harsh measures to suppress real enemies against the State. For this purpose, the most trusted police officers of Diwan, Vaithanada Aiyar and Parthasarathy Ayankar, were deputed to crush the working class agitation. The police officers met all the prominent landlords and industrialists in Shertallai tourist bungalow and made discussions with them. Their main intention was to make counter-movement against the growing working class solidarity in the State. They organised rowdies and *goondas* who started attacking the union leaders, women labourers and party offices. The government officials and the state machinery completely sided with the landlords for organising *goondas* against the trade union movement.[24] The trade unions demanded the proper distribution of food, clothes and kerosene through fair shops and pleaded for the establishment of public distribution system. Beside these, they demanded the suppression of rowdies, employment to all, leave bonuses to all, etc.

But the landlords and factory owners made provocative moves towards the labourers. Anthraper, a local State Congress leader and also a prominent landlord, organised 1000 rowdies and started assaults and attacks on workers and working class families. Morris, a factory owner, assaulted the coir factory workers continuously for ten days. Another landlord, named Cocho, evicted the tenants from his land at the time of harvesting and raised the *pattam* (revenue) indiscriminately. The rowdies under the leadership of Raman attacked labourers' houses and abused women workers at Thaikkal and Kadakkarapilly. At last, the laboures resented against these and collided with rowdies and gang leader Raman was killed in the encounter.[25] Next day, the army seized the Shertallai coir factory workers union office and started lathi charge through the streets of Ponnanvelly market. Labour union leaders were arrested, files and documents were destroyed and red flags were removed from union office.[26]

The whole area was in constant state of fear and workers left their houses and the reign of terror unleashed by the state-sponsored anti-social elements induced the trade unions and Communist Party to start camps for their self-defence. The government and the Diwan, Sir C.P. Ramaswamy Aiyer, accused "the Communists were creating troubles in the interior." The Travancore Peoples Association of Bombay described the prevailing situation in Travancore, "A naked police rule exists in the State of Travancore today. The batons of reserve police and rifles of military had been seen in many parts of the State. At Alleppey and Shertallai, shooting has already been started by military. The government finds faults with Communists for their military high-handedness, in fact the government alone is responsible for all the tragedy. Police is at perfect liberty to enter into any house and even beat up anybody they like, women and children are not spared."[27]

The A.T.T.U.C. declared a one day strike on 15th September 1946 against the mounting repression let loose by government and landlords. It was a grand success and a general meeting of all trade unions in the State was convened on 25 September 1946 in Alleppey to discuss the future course of action. The meeting was attended by 83 delegates representing 55 trade unions.[28] Apart from the representatives of various unions, the veteran State Congress leader C. Kesavan also participated in the conference. He was very much excited by the unity of labourers and declared that "American Model of Reforms is not acceptable with any cause." The general consensus was to start a general strike on any day after October 12, 1946. The State Congress Working Committee gave two more weeks to Pattom Thanupillai to make discussions with Diwan. Therefore, the general meeting of the trade unions decided to start the general strike only after the meeting of State Congress.

Meanwhile the government arranged a tripartite conference consisting of industrialists, officials and labour union leaders at the official residence of Diwan. T.V. Thomas and N. Sreekantan Nair attended the conference on behalf of A.T.T.U.C. The Diwan discussed with them almost all the issues related to labour like annual bonus, deferred wages, holidays with pay, reduction of hours of work, fixation of minimum wages, labour welfare schemes, enquiry into the miserable conditions of labour in plantations, etc.[29] After the tripartite conference, Diwan decided to receive the A.T.T.U.C. leaders in Bhakti Vilas. T.V. Thomas attended the exclusive meeting with Diwan. He wanted an assurance from the side of labourers to support the American Model of Reforms and not to give any support to the State Congress in the struggle for responsible government. T.V. Thomas categorically rejected the demand made by Diwan and proclaimed that the trade unions would give active support to the State Congress in the struggle for responsible government.

The infuriated Diwan promulgated the Emergency Provision Act on 1 October, 1946. The Travancore People Association of Bombay described the situation, "A state of emergency has been declared in Travancore. C.P. Ramaswamy Aiyar has taken up powers of life and death over 61 lakhs of Travancoreans." C. Kesavan described the regulation as "one that regulated all, except air and water."[30] Before his arrest, he made a clarion call to the State Congress to mobilise all the democratic forces of the State for a final struggle. The State Congress Working Committee met as per the earlier decision on 9 October and took no action regarding the further struggle against American Model Constitutional Reforms. On 13 October 1946, the representatives of labour unions met in Alleppey and decided to start the general strike and constituted an action committee to lead the struggle.[31]

Meanwhile, the A.T.T.U.C. submitted a charter of 27 demands before the government on 20 October 1946. Apart from the economic character of demands, A.T.T.U.C. necessitated the release of political prisoners and detainees, withdrawal of army from Alleppey, termination of Diwan rule, elected assembly on the basis of adult franchise, end of Raja's rule, abolition of all posts carrying a salary of more than 500 rupees per month, prohibition of eviction of tenants, etc.[32] The government response to these was the deployment of more military and police force in Alleppey and adjacent areas. The government viewed the general strike as a challenge to the organised authority of the State. The government made it clear that "any strike at the instance of any political party as a means of labour trying to change the form of government could not be countenanced and decided to take all necessary action to deal with the strike."[33]

The Communist Party and trade unions also made preparations for the final struggle and an action committee was constituted with K.V. Pathrose as convener. Volunteer camps had been set up in Vayalar, Punnapra, Mararikulam, Olathala, Kalavancode, Parur, Menessary, Port Vadekkal, Thumboli, Varakkad, Kannarkad, Chungam, Kanjiramchira, etc. The Diwan knew the preparatory works done by the working class and Communist Party. He ordered the arrest of trade union leaders and raiding of the union offices.

As per the earlier decision, T.V. Thomas called for a general strike which started on 22 October, 1946. The entire labour force of coastal area from Arur to Quilon, consisting of 70,000 workers, had gone to strike for an indefinite period.[34] On the birthday of Maharaja on 24 October, the striking workers attacked the Punnapra Reserve Police camp, which was started earlier to look after the Communist activities. This police camp had given protection to prominent landlords of that area and monitored the counter movement started by the landlords and *goondas* against the working class in this region.[35] The police inspector asked them to disperse peacefully but the reply of the labourers was the dismissal of the repressive police camp. The police opened fire towards the mob and, as instructed earlier, the labourers lay down on the earth and crawled towards the police and attacked them with crude lances, sickles, stones, arecanut spears, axes, bamboo sticks, etc. The official record speaks that 27 persons were killed as a result of police firing at Punnapra.[36]

Faced with unprecedented violence in Punnapra, the government proclaimed martial law on 25 October, 1946 and Shertallai and Amballapuzha Thalukhs were brought under its purview. Again there were direct confrontations between the labourers and military forces at Mararikulam, Menessary and Olthala places. The death toll at these two places was roughly 130 volunteers as calculated by the Communist Party.[37] The most important and nerve centre of Communist activities was Vayalar and it was this camp, which coordinated and directed the activities of other camps. The position of Vayalar was very conspicuous because it was surrounded by water on three sides.[38] On 27

October, 1946, the military attacked the Vayalar camp with modern sophisticated weapons like stenguns and ammunitions. Indiscriminate shooting was done by military comprising of 400 men against the 200 volunteers in the camp. The resistance of the labourers with rude weapons also failed against the heavily armed state machinery. Within a short time, the military destroyed all the volunteer camps and liberated the areas under the Communist influences. In Punnapra, the dead bodies of the volunteers were tied in coconut leaves and loaded by *thottis,* (scavangers) into lorries and poured with petrol and set in to fire. In Vayalar, the dead bodies and semi-wounded labours were dumped into a well and raised by a heap of soil.[39] The Travancore State Congress completely kept aloof from the Punnapra- Vayalar struggle and had not given any support to the working class families in the affected areas. In addition to this, the State Congress Enquiry Committee also justified the promulgation of martial law in the taluks and concluded that there was no indiscriminate shooting from the part of the State forces.[40]

The Diwan, Sir C.P. Ramaswamy Aiyar, and his government were very much delighted by the suppression of the Communists and the working class in the State of Travancore. He blamed the Communist Party and its leaders for their miscalculated political adventure and accused the party that before the revolt "the Communist Party gave assurance to the workers to distribute 13/12 cents of land to each."[41]

The number of persons, who lost their lives in the encounter, is still a very controversial issue in the history of the State. The party sources put the death toll as 500,[42] Ani Mascrine, a prominent State Congress leader, expressed her view that 7000 labourers lost their lives.[43] The Government of Travancore put the death toll as 190 persons.[44] The Travancore Peoples Association described the struggle as "What is taking place in Travancore today is Hitlerite oppression and military rule, on the one hand, and heroic resistance of a determined courageous and organised people, on the other. The epic battles can only be compared with Ballia and Sattara of 1942. The people of Travancore are writing history with their blood."[45] All Communist organisations were declared unlawful and the innocent labourers were subjected to notorious treatment. The unions, which participated in the violent activity consisting of 34 cases, were dealt with and they have been charged for acts of violence, including war against the Maharaja.

For a short time, the government and the Diwan were able to suppress the working class unity in the State. But his motive to crush working class solidarity and contain Communist influences among the vivid sections of society never materialised. The working class resurrected with great labour force within a year. Even today, many prominent historians and political parties in the state are not in a position to admit the Punnapra-Vayalar as a part of freedom struggle and hold the view that it was an avoidable tragedy. The Government of India accepted it as a part of freedom struggle only in 1997. As a matter of fact, it became necessary for the working class to fight against the state terrorism and to attain the responsible government in the state with their own means. There are numerous historical interpretations regarding the nature of the struggle waged by the working class in the State of Travancore and its role in the struggle for responsible government.

The most conspicuous factor, which worked behind the acceleration of the responsible government in Travancore, was the martyrdom of the innocent workers from the Punnapra-Vayalar region. It was highly politically suicidal to C.P. Ramaswamy Aiyar and within a short time he left the State with a wounded nose. The Punnapra-Vayalar struggle helped the Communist Party a lot in the future electoral politics and even today remains a great inspirational factor for millions of people in the country.

## References


1. S. Ramachandran Nair, *Democracy and Power : Electoral Politics in Kerala*, (Manak, New Delhi 2013), p. 6.
2. Nagam Aiya, *Travancore State Manual*, Vol. 3, Gazetteers Department, (Government of Kerala, Trivandrum 1999), p. 1.
3. *Report of Industries of Travancore, 1939-1940*, Government of Travancore, p. 82, Kerala State Archives, Trivandrum (hereafter K.S.A.).
4. For further details about Sir C.P. Ramaswamy Aiyar's and Earl Winterton's statement, Consult *Prohibited writings of Freedom Fighters*, (State Archives Department, Trivandrum 2007) , p. 52.
5. Parliamentary Debates, House of Commons, 21 February, 1938, Vol. 332, p. 6, cited in S. Raimon ed., *History of Freedom Movement in Kerala,* (State Archives Department, Trivandrum, 2006), p. 44.
6. Travancore State Congress President Pattom Thanu Pillai's Statement to the Press, *File No. 59 / 3, Political Department*, National Archives of India, New Delhi.
7. Report of the Inspector General of Police to Chief Secretary to Government, 11th March 1942, *Confidential Section File No. 420 / 44*, KSA, Trivandrum.

8. Ramachandran Nair, S., "Freedom Struggle and Labour Movement in Travancore", in Charles Dias, (ed.), *Kerala Spectrum: Aspects of Cultural Inheritance*, (Concept, Ernakulum 2007), pp. 1-8.
9. N.E. Balaram, *Keralathile Communist Prasthanam*, (Prabhat Book House, Trivandrum, 1973), p. 39.
10. *Travancore Economic Depression Committee Report*, Government of Travancore 1931, Kerala State Archives, Trivandrum, p. 23.
11. *Ibid.*, pp. 24-29.
12. *100 Years of Legislative Bodies in Kerala 1888-1988, Centenary Souvenir*, Government of Kerala, 1988, Trivandrum, pp. 487-48.
13. For details see *Proceedings of Sri Mulam Assembly,* Vol. XIX, No. 4, 1942, Kerala State Archives, Trivandrum, pp. 256-257.
14. Police Report from I.G. to Chief Secretary, 22 January, 1942, *Confidential Section, File No. 469/44*, KSA, Trivandrum.
15. Report of I.G. to Chief Secretary, 28th December, 1940, *Confidential Section, File No. 740/47*, KSA, Trivandrum.
16. *Proceedings of Sri Mulam Assembly,* Vol. XIX, No. 4, 1942, KSA, Trivandrum.
17. For further details see Fortnightly Reports, Government of Travancore, *Confidential Section File No.130/40*, KSA, Trivandrum.
18. *Arunodhayam Famine Special Magazine*, Proscribed by Travancore State Government available in Confidential Section, File No. 712/44, KSA, Trivandrum.
19. Letter from Personal Secretary to Diwan Sir C.P. Ramaswamy Aiyer, *Confidential Section File No. 552/46*, KSA, Trivandrum.
20. Dewans statement in Sri Mulam Assembly for details consults *Proceedings of Sri Mulam Assembly, op. cit.* p. 36.
21. N. Sreekantan Nair *Vanchikapeteta Venad*, 1947, Trivandrum, p. 40.

22. *Travancore Government Press Comminique,16 Januvary, 1946*, KSA, Trivandrum.
23. Puthupally Raghavan, *R. Sughathan: A Political Biography*, Current Books, Kottayam, 1999, p. 175.
24. Pamphlet Issued by All Travancore Trade Union Congress, (ATTUC), *Confidential Section File No. 739/46*, KSA, Trivandrum.
25. *Ibid.*
26. *The Report of All Kerala Student Congress, Confidential Section File No.11/47*, KSA, Trivandrum.
27. Bulletin of the Travancore Peoples Association Bombay, No. 1, *Confidential Section File No. 767/47*, KSA, Trivandrum.
28. Puthupally Raghavan, *op. cit*, pp. 140-142.
29. Notes on the Agenda of Tripartite Labour Conference, October, 7-8, 1946, *Confidential Section File No. 370/48*, KSA, Trivandrum.
30. Speech of State Congress Leader, C. Kesavan, available in *Confidential Section File No.767/46*, KSA, Trivandrum.
31. Puthupally Raghavan, *Viplavasmranakal* (Malayalam), Memoir, Part. III, DC Books, Kottayam, 1992-1996, p. 45.
32. For details see circular of the All Travancore Trade Union Congress, *Confidential Section File No. 805/46*, KSA, Trivandrum.
33. *Travancore Information and Listener,* Vol. VI, No. 3, November 1946, Kerala Studies Section, Kerala University Library, Trivandrum, p. 19.
34. *Confidential Section File No. 767/46*, KSA, Trivandrum.
35. *Travancore Information and Listener,* Vol. VI, No. 5, Januvary 1947, Kerala Studies Section, Kerala University Library, Trivandrum, p. 7.
36. Police Report, *Confidential Section File. No.774/46,* KSA, Trivandrum.

37. K.C. George, *Punnapra Vayalar*, Prabhat Book House, Trivandrum, 1972, pp. 167-168.
38. Kattakada Divakaran, *Keraliyee Gramangalilude*, Sahitya Pravarthaka Co-operative Society, Kottayam, 1968, p. 225.
39. History Association (compl.), *Kerala History*, Ernakulam, 1974, p. 220.
40. Report of the Special Subcommittee appointed by the Travancore State Congress, *C.S. File No. 82/47*, KSA, Trivandrum.
41. For further details see C.P. Ramaswamy Iyer's interview with Associated Press of India in *Travancore Information and Listener,* Vol. VI, No. 4, December 1946, Kerala Studies Section, Kerala University Library, Trivandrum, p. 46.
42. K.C. George, Punnapra Vayalar, *op. cit.*, Preface, (iii).
43. Statement of Ani Mascrine in *Malabar Herald*, November 9, 1946, KSA, Trivandrum.
44. Travancore Information and Listener, *op. cit.*, p. 38.
45. Select Documents in Freedom Struggle in Kerala, S. Raimon ed., *History of Freedom Movement in Kerala*, (State Archives Department, Trivandrum, 2006), p. 44.

# 9

# Labour and the Anti-colonial Struggle in French India

*A. Suresh*

## Introduction

French India, of five settlements and eleven *loges* comprising an area of little over 500 sq. kms, was under the control of the French imperialism for more than two centuries. The natives lost their political, economic and socio-cultural rights under the colonial yoke and, especially the working class felt the heat of the colonial exploitation more. A strong labour movement was started in French India by early twentieth century, with the aim of protecting and promoting the class interests of the industrial and agricultural labour. After lot of efforts and sacrifices on the part of the working class, the French colonial masters and the European capitalists relented in the end. They extended progressive labour rights to their colonies in India, which was considered as something more progressive than the then prevailing Asian standards. Soon, the working class clamoured for political independence from the French colonial masters, who resorted to suppress the movement and to weaken it through encouraging division among the nationalist elements. In the end, the French Indians succeeded in getting their territories transferred to the Indian Union. As such, the working class had played a significant role in the anti-colonial struggle against the French rule in India. The present paper aims to study and analyse the role played by the working class in awakening the class and political consciousness among the French Indians and their stand on the anti-colonial struggle in French India.

## Condition of the Labour in French India

In the early twentieth century, French India had an overwhelming agrarian economy and society. More than 80 per cent of the region's inhabitants lived in rural areas, and four out of every five of them depended directly on agriculture for their livelihood. Within the village, three social levels can be distinguished, albeit with imprecise boundaries. At the top were landlords and rich peasants[1] beneath them were middle peasants; and at the bottom were poor agricultural labourers. The poor agricultural labourers were characteristically low castes, *Pariahs* and *Vannias* and comprised around 40 per cent of the population. The agricultural labourers were called *Padial* in Pondicherry[2] and were "faithfully attached to their masters who had the right of life and death on them."[3] Though most agricultural labourers belonged to the low-caste *Pariah*, some belonged to other castes as well (e.g. the poorest *Retty)*. The agricultural labourers depended wholly or partially on the sale of their labour for their survival. They were free workers on daily wages and they worked also for daily wages in the field of land owners. Thus, one can say that the position of the coolies, *padials* and *pannaiyals* was not any better in the village or rural society as they had to be obedient to their masters. According to one observer:

"The working condition of agricultural labourers was rigorous. The whole day the labourer had to work in the field of master. There were two main breaks from which the worker managed to take a little time for rest when his master did not observe him. On the other hand, many workers were often obliged to work beyond the stipulated hours. As he approached the master's house at the end of the day to collect his daily wages (*Padi*), he may be asked to look after the cattle for a while or he would be sent out on an errand, to shops or to buy anything from the market centres. Only a few workers could refuse such a command as there was risk of losing their job. Besides, they had no good dress to wear, they had no good huts...they had no proper food, they ate low nutrition food. The men who worked for bonded labour moved with the bullocks of their masters than with the human members of their family. They took it for granted that if they were ready to nurse their wife and children in times of illness, they would give the same care to the animals of their masters."[4]

The wages, given to the labourers, were insufficient. Generally, for ploughing 1¼ rupees was paid; for general works only ½ rupee was paid; women workers were only paid ¼ rupee for transplanting and weeding. Sometimes ½ rupee was paid for the general or domestic works. The working hours per day were more than 12 hours, but they were not given proper wages. If the master was wealthy and having the support of government authorities, the working hours and the wages were not taken into consideration.[5] The wages of women were less than the wages of men. Though the French were the first to sing-up the slogans, 'Liberty', 'Equality', and 'Fraternity', and extended the citizenship of France to all the inhabitants of their settlements, they kept silent in India without taking much interest in reconstruction of the Indian peasantry. As the French were colonialists, they did not try to improve the peasantry. Instead, they swindled income from the peasantry.

Industries also made a contribution to the French India economy and provided more employment opportunities for the native population, mostly to weavers, dyers and artisans. Industrialisation of France in the mid-nineteenth century influenced French India as well. Despite heavy pressure on import of cloth from French India in France, the Méline Laws of 11 January 1892 made some relaxation by exempting duties for the *guinées* of Pondicherry at their entry in France. The products of a French colony exported to another French colony was exempted from undergoing any custom duties.[6] This law struck a happy note in French India and it offered new perspectives, particularly in the textile industry. The granting of the colonial market in France and in the French colonies encouraged capitals, especially from British industrialists, to build powerful factories of cotton fabrics in Pondicherry and a jute mill in Chandernagore. Four cotton mills started functioning in Pondicherry: (i) *Society Anonyme Savanna* or *Swadeshi* Mill was established in 1828, (ii) *Etablissement textile de* Modéliarpeth or Enny Mill was established in 1858, (iii) Rodier Mill or Anglo-French Textile Ltd., was established in 1899, and (iv) *Filature et Tissage Gaebelé* at Kossapalayam. Altogether these mills possessed 1,980 looms and 85,376 spindles, and employed about 8,000 labourers at the turn of the nineteenth century. These mills produced 5,000 tonnes of export quality cotton clothes annually and Pondicherry exported 8,210 balls of *guinées* per year on the average between 1902 and

1913. Usually two kinds of cloth were produced in these mills. The first was *Sylas,*[7] exported to south-eastern countries like Malaysia, and the second was *'guinées bleus'*, made of cotton and dyed with indigo, which had a preferential and protected market in the French overseas colonies in Africa. Apart from this, about 6,968 traditional handlooms in Muthialpet area in Pondicherry produced *Sylas* cloth. Gondalpara jute mill in Chandernagore too came into existence in the due course of time. Big export enterprises like Ralley Brothers, Volkar and East Asiatic Company too were present at Pondicherry. However, in the other French Indian settlements like Karaikal, Yanam and Mahe, there was no industrialisation of significance.

The following table shows the group of working class population in each settlement, profession-wise:

**Table 1. Working Class Population in French India as in 1930**

| *Professional Groups* | *Pondicherry* | *Karaikal* | *Chandernagore* | *Mahe* | *Yanam* |
|---|---|---|---|---|---|
| Textile Mill Workers | 8,100 | — | 5000 | — | — |
| Agriculturalists | 30,000 | 15,000 | — | 4000 | 2,000 |
| Textile Craftsmen | 10,000 | 6000 | — | 300 | 300 |
| Fisher Men | 3,000 | 600 | — | 100 | — |
| Others | 5,000 | 1,200 | 2,000 | 200 | 100 |

*Source:* Annuaire pour l'Inde française, 1931.

Social condition in French India became more complex as Pondicherry got modernised due to starting of modern industries. The starting of these mills led to the emergence of an industrial working class in Pondicherry. There was steady increase of migration from rural to urban areas as well as population from British India. These industries recruited 8,000 to 10,000 labourers at the turn of the nineteenth century and the working class population was largely concentrated in Olgarat, Modaliarpet and Kossapalayam (outskirts of Pondicherry town). A good number of working class population was found at Chandernagore as well, where a jute mill was situated.[8] Most of the mill workers at that time belonged to the low-castes and untouchables. The higher castes ignored the mill jobs which were considered as polluted, whereas the deprived castes having no other source for the survival took up mill jobs. While the modern textile mills came into existence and grew in number, the condition of weavers and the artisans who depended for their livelihood on handmade textiles declined. As in British India, the French rulers dumped the machine made textile in the Indian market. The consequence of this was disastrous for the Indian weavers who consequently suffered downward mobility in the economic hierarchy. Due to their rural background, illiteracy and little bargaining power, and their 'superstition and ignorance', they were employed as forced, bonded, and child labourers. Further the working conditions of labourers were bad. For instance, the mill workers had to work 12 to 14 hours per day and compulsorily 24 days in a month. They had to work all the days including Sunday, there was no security of job, and their wages were relatively very low.[9] In an article published in the '*Bulletin du comité de l'Asie française*' in 1905 under the title "*l'agriculture et l'industrie dans l'Inde française*", Doctor Charles Valentino exposed the living conditions of the labourers in the mills in the following manner:

> "*La situation des ouvriers est intolérable. Sans parler de la situation des adultes, dont les salaires*

*sont souvent trop petits pour l'énorme travail exigé, il convient d'appeler l'attention du gouvernement sur l'exploitation des enfants, laquelle ne connaît pas de bornes. On fait travailler dans ces filatures, dont la température atteint souvent jusqu'à 47° et dans lesquelles aucune disposition sanitaire n'est prise, ni pour aspirer les poussières, ni pour ventiler, des enfants de dix, neuf et même huit ans, pendant onze heures, et on leur donne comme salaire quotidien de deux à trois sous".*[10]

Valentino further noticed the attitudes of the investors of British India,

*"il fait bien se rendre compte (...) que les directeurs anglais de l'usine Rodier ne sont pas venus mettre leur usine sur notre territoire pour le plaisir de faire gagner nos populations, mais, précisément, pour échapper aux obligations anglaises et augmenter par la leurs bénéfices".*[11]

Another condemnation was the political use of labourers. With the endowment of political institutions and universal suffrage in the late nineteenth century French India, in the rural communes the agricultural labourers were used as voting mass for *Rettys* and *Vellajas*; in the urban areas labourers were used for political purpose. The Indian party accused the leading industrialists and chiefs of the pro-French party Henri Gaebelé and Ernest Cornet for exploiting Indians by bringing *Pariahs* to work in their mills to vote for the party.[12] As such the labourer lived under the constant threat of dismissal if they agitated against the mill management. Whenever workers started an agitation, the mill management put it down with the help of local police and French administration. Moreover, during this period their attempt to improve their conditions rarely met with success. The uselessness and failure of the open professional schools established in 1896 were also quite obvious. The French had established industrial schools. However, because manual labour was not well regarded in India, the students whom these schools recruited were also of the lower castes. They were in fact, not able to compete with those who had hereditary training. As such the low caste labourers were thus condemned to be workers of inferior quality and pushed into unskilled labour. Moreover, physical weakening of the body, which resulted from malnutrition and from an excess of alcoholic drinks and constrained difficult living conditions, made them vulnerable to the onslaught of epidemics.[13] These contradictions helped in enhancing opposition to French colonial rule. Among all the working sections of French India, like textile workers, agricultural labourers, handloom weavers, household workers, seashore labourers, toddy tappers and others, the textile workers were the first to organise their struggle against exploitation of the mill owners and French colonialism in Pondicherry.[14]

## Emergence of Anti-colonialism

During the post-World War I period, the French administration had to face the problem of challenge against its authority as the growth of Indian nationalism affected the native population of French India. The French administrators followed the draconian methods of suppression and oppression, with the aid of the decrees promulgated during the war time, to stamp out the seeds of Indian nationalism from the soil of French Indian settlements. Thus, the ideological basis of Indian nationalism was taking deep roots even in the early twentieth century. It is a unique factor that mass mobilisation in the French settlements was achieved through labour unrest. The labour force in the textile mills in Pondicherry had a substantial population and was experienced enough to form the basis of a mass movement against the mill management and French colonial rule. Though sporadic incidents of labour unrest were witnessed even by the turn of the 1880s in the four textile mills of Pondicherry, organised form of protest came into existence only in the 1920s.[15]

The World War I caused severe shortage in the supply of cotton for the mills in Pondicherry. The imports of bad quality cotton increased weavers' work burden and the amount of damaged product. Consequently, the mill managements began to impose fine on damaged products.[16] So the only option presented to the labourers was to quit their job or revolt against the managements. Series of strikes were organised in the 1920s demanding for better conditions: (i) an increase in their wages; (ii) reduction of working hours; (iii) weekly holidays, and (iv) improved sanitary conditions.[17] The journals in Pondicherry regularly published articles condemning the arrogant mentality of the mill management and calling on the workers to organise themselves into trade union. It advised the mill workers to demand reduction of working hours and other facilities enjoyed by their counterparts in France.[18] The occurrence of famine[19] in 1916 made a long-term impact on the labourers' living conditions. With the intervention of French administration, the mill management agreed to increase the wages a little and to supply rice at a concessioned rate. They also ensured the suspension of all the fines imposed on the labourers. A labour fund was established in the mills to look after the welfare of the labourers.[20] The years from 1920 to 1925 constituted the worst period for labourers in the mills. The misappropriation of labour fund and the political rivalries established in the mills caused frequent strikes, lockouts and violence in the mills. The police force was frequently used to threaten the labourers. In February 1920, there were clashes between the labourers and the police. There was also a clash between the management and the labourers in the Savana and Anglo-French mills. In this violence, two workers were killed, many were arrested and the labourers were forced to take refuge in British India.[21] The *Morning Post* condemned this incident and accused the investors of exploiting the labour force in Pondicherry. The French Indian deputy Paul Bluysen ordered an enquiry into the incident. Following this incident, a committee was set up, including labour leaders and mill managements, to form 14 rules and regulations of the mills.[22] In the absence of 'proper labour protection laws', the mill managements continued to exploit the labour force in Pondicherry.

**Working Class Movement in 1930's**

The changing socio-political atmosphere clearly affected the course of the labour movement in Pondicherry. In any society, the youth and the working class always spearhead any political and socio-economic movement and the labour population of French India was no exception to this general rule. The Civil Disobedience Movement launched in 1930s opened the eyes of the French Indian youth. This helped in awakening the political and social consciousness among the people, which resulted in the demand for social reforms and for the end of alien rule in India. The workers were attracted by an individual leader, a group of leaders or by social organisations like 'French India Youth Association' and *'Harijan Seva Sangh'*. In September 1931, a French India Labour Conference was held at Odiyansalai *maidan* in Pondicherry. It was arranged at the initiative of Selvaraju Chettiar by his followers. Leaders from Madras Presidency like P. Subburayan and Kanaga Sankara Kannappan addressed the conference. This conference was the first labour conference in the history of French India.[23] In the absence of labourers' laws, the French Indian administration did not come forward to solve the workers' problems. The members instigated the workers to form secret unions to fight for their rights.[24] These committees began to function indirectly and took important decisions regarding their struggle against the management to improve their working conditions.

The worldwide economic depression in 1930s affected the textile productions in French India by (i) the imposition of customs barriers; (ii) cut-throat competition; and (iii) decline of overseas market for textile products leading to decline in the demand for cotton cloths from Pondicherry.[25] For the above reasons, the mill managements took measures to reduce their cost of production. This was done through retrenchment of workers and through reduction of their wages. The mill workers organised a series of strikes and lockouts and put forward their legitimate demands. In February 1935, 3000 workers of the Savana mill started an agitation demanding increase in wages and decrease in the working hours. They succeeded in wresting an increase in daily wages from three to six *annas* and a reduction in the working hours from 12 or 14 to 10 hours. They also demanded that women should not be asked to work during night times and they should be given one month paid leaves with half pay during confinement. There was also a demand for ban on employment of children below 14 years of age.[26] With the active backing of the French Indian authorities, the mill owners resorted to dismiss the leaders and active participants of the working class movement. However, in the end, they had to revoke their earlier orders to appease the working classes.

Meanwhile, in June 1936, *Front Populaire* headed by Leon Blum, consisting of Communists and Socialists, formed a coalition government in France. This pro-(left) Communist government in France aroused great expectations among the workers of the mills in French India. In this hope in June 1936, the mill workers resumed their movement clamouring for the right to form into labour unions, eight hours work, the right to collective bargaining, increase in wages and weekly holidays. The Governor initially accepted to promulgate all progressive labour legislations after due consultation with the French Government and requested the labour leaders to stop their agitation. But he failed to fulfil his promise by the end of the stipulated period and the labour leaders had to resort to their agitation. The workers went on 'stay in-strike' again on 25 and 26 July 1936. Consequently, the situation became tense. The Governor, Léon Solomiac (1934-1936), sent the French police to control the situation. A worker of the Rodier mill was killed in the violence. The police then moved to the Savanna mill, where the situation had become tense due to spreading of the news that a worker had been killed in the Rodier mill. In order to control the situation, the governor gave shooting order to the police. It resulted in the killing of twelve workers and some workers were severely injured.[27] In order to meet the situation and to meet the increasing militancy of the labour movement, the third company of the eleventh regiment of *Infanterie Coloniale* was brought to Pondicherry. It stayed on up to 1939.[28]

The tragedy of 1936 was reported to France. Paris ordered an immediate enquiry and took action. The French Indian Governor, Léon Solomiac, was called back to France. Justin Godart, the senator representing French India, came to Pondicherry as a special delegate of workers in French India. He submitted a report to the Government of France. On the basis of his recommendations, the coalition government of France introduced a worker's law by the Decree of sixth April 1937.[29] The law reduced the working hour to eight, abolished child labour, granted weekly holidays, women workers were made eligible to take eight weeks of maternity leave and, most importantly, the law recognised the formation of workers unions in industrial organisations.[30] Thus the workers movement in French India marched one step ahead of similar movements in Asia so far as the issue of working hours was concerned. The labour leaders like Subbiah maintained contacts with Nehru, a trade union leader in his own right, who assisted them to gain contacts with their comrades in France. This enabled the former in securing their helping hand in their on-going struggle for protecting labour rights and to get the liberal and progressive labour laws of France introduced and implemented in the French Indian settlements.[31] The victory, achieved by the textile workers, had inspired other sections of the working class to form their own associations. The 'Agricultural Society of French India' was started in 1943, with the efforts of M.R. Pandurangan and V. Subbiah who rendered their services for the development of agriculturalists. It was first started in the name of 'French Indian Kisan Sabha'. The mode of this organisation was to protect the agricultural labourers from the oppression of the big land owners and the French Government. This organisation was very similar to the organisation which followed the rules and regulations of the All India Kisan Sabha (AIKS). The French Indian Kisan Sabha fought for reducing the tax burden of the peasants, land to the tillers, etc., as the major resolutions and spoke of provision of irrigation facilities, fair price of cotton, sugarcane and other commercial crops as the minor resolutions.[32] This peasant movement was dominated by the Leftists who had two types of pulls. One was the ideological pull which made the organisation resolve to fight for poor peasants, landless tenants and other labourers, etc., on the other hand, there was a political pull to get ahead of the Congress, the ruling party and the government in British India. The intensification of labour movement had its impact on the politics in French India.

## Political Struggle against Colonial Domination

In the twentieth century, French India was influenced more and more by the growing Indian nationalism, official programmes of the Indian National Congress and the activities of nationalist leaders. In line with nationalist tendencies, the Mahajana Party was established in 1937, by V. Subbiah and other politically volatile elements like Marie Savary, Dorairaj and Purushotama Reddiar and they wanted to do away with the inordinate power enjoyed by the Governor of French India on the strength of the *Ordonnance organique*, to remove the existing anomaly of two-list voter system and to ensure the conduct of free and fair elections.[33]

Subsequently, branches of Mahajana Party were established in the other French Indian settlements as well.

In the municipal elections of May 2, 1937, the Franco-Hindu Party, which was supported by the French Indian authorities, with their police and administrative machinery, and the Mahajana Party contested. Although the latter could gain the popular support of agricultural and industrial labourers, through sheer muscle power and governmental support, the Franco-Hindu Party was declared elected and Mahajana Party disputed the veracity of the results. The ruling party used police and its *goonda* elements to terrorise all remnants of opposition and the labour leaders. The mill workers had to fight pitched battles with them and in the end, the government had to come to terms with the working class leaders. However, Mahajana Party lost even in the elections for the *Conseil general* (General Council), which were held on October 10, 1937, due to the political manoeuvre of Crocicchia, the then Governor of French India.

Mahajana Party and other democratic elements retaliated by launching a Non-co-operation Movement. They established *Gram Panchayats*, sealed the civil registries and government offices, disregarded the authority and orders of the police and judiciary and started running a parallel government.[34] As part of the no-tax campaign, the people refused to pay taxes to the government. The French Indian administration came to a standstill. Moreover, the people demonstrated in front of the houses of the Municipal Councillors, who were declared elected by the government and demanded their immediate resignation. As a result, few councillors resigned their office. The government had to come to terms with the popular leaders and agree to conduct free and fair elections within six months period.

About this time, the Popular Front Government in France was dissolved and the reactionary Radical Socialist Party came to power on April 16, 1938. As a fallout, the French Indian authorities threw their assurances in the wind. They resorted to the policy of repression against the workers. A French army battalion was brought from Indo-China to Pondicherry to suppress any political agitation. Several mass leaders were imprisoned. *Gram Panchayats* organised earlier and village libraries were destroyed. Thousands of people had to leave Pondicherry and take asylum in the surrounding Indian territories. The use of force proved to be counter-productive and resulted in the eruption of political violence. There was an unsuccessful attempt on the life of Joseph David, one of the leaders of the ruling Franco-Hindu Party. Selvarajulu Chettiar, another pro-French leader, who led the suppression of the working class elements, was assassinated by Ramaiah, a worker of Savana mill, on December 16, 1938.[35]

The French India Communist Party came into existence in early 1940s, and along with other progressive democratic forces it formed the National Democratic Front (NDF), which demanded the right to have self-rule, adult suffrage to both men and women and the introduction of fundamental and democratic rights to the colonies. When the Nazi army entered into the war with Russia in June 1941, the French India Communist Party launched its campaign against Nazi Germany and joined hands with other democratic forces in forming a branch of Combat[36] at Pondicherry in April

1944, and V. Subbiah was elected as its Chairman. However, Louis Bonvin, the then Governor of Pondicherry, charged him as an undesirable element and expelled him from the French Indian settlements.

In 1944, D. Zivarattinam, the representative of the French India in the Consultative Assembly in Paris, demanded a single list of voters and called for the abolition of the reserved seats or separate electorates for the Europeans and their descendants. On August 3, 1945, the separate electorates were abolished and a single list of voters came into force in the French colonies in India. The Fourth Republic of France under General de Gaulle revoked the expulsion order against V. Subbiah on September 11, 1945 and allowed him to continue to work at Pondicherry. This political change in France and in the French Indian settlements augured well for the freedom movement in the following years.

## Role of Working Class in the Liberation Movement in French India

In the Municipal elections held on June 23, 1946, in the five French Indian territories, on the basis of universal adult franchise and a single electoral list, the NDF triumphed. It captured power in all the 22 Municipal Councils of French India, winning 101 out of 122 municipal seats and its candidates were elected as Mayors.[37] Its election manifesto proclaimed in favour of French India remaining fully a self-governing national unit within the French Republic (*Communaute Française Republicaine*) and demanded adequate representation for French India in the representative institutions to be newly formed in France. Even in the elections held to elect a member to the National Assembly in Paris on November 10, 1946, the candidate of NDF, Lambert Saravane, a Professor of French at the

Colonial College, had triumphed. In the elections for the new *Assemblée Representative* (Representative Assembly) held on December 15, 1946 also, the NDF won 34 seats out of 44. On January 26, 1947, for the first time, two Indian candidates of the NDF were elected to the Senate in Paris by the Representative Assembly of Pondicherry.[38]

However, by the end of 1946, there was a split among the constituents of the Front and some moderates, who were estranged by the radical policies of the French India Communist Party, formed the French India National Congress and All French India Congress.[39] On January 1, 1947, another moderate leader, S.R. Subramanyam, organised the Congress Socialist Party to continue the struggle for the freedom of French Indian settlements.

In January 1947, there was a change in the stand of the NDF. While it stood for the status of a self-governing national unit within the French Republic in 1946, now it started clamouring for *Purna Swaraj* (complete independence) and for immediate merger with the Indian Union. The leaders of the Front presented similar demand for independence to Maurice Moutet, the then French Overseas Minister, when he visited Pondicherry on his way back from Indo-China. Moutet seemed to be evasive on the question of independence.

The nationalist elements of Pondicherry observed February 17, 1947 as the first anniversary of the rebellion of the Naval Cadets at Bombay. More than 10,000 workers, peasants, students and others took a procession in Pondicherry. A peaceful *bandh* was also organised, and mills, shops and educational institutions remained closed. The police and pro-French *goonda* elements obstructed the processionists by pelting stones and by spraying boiled oil on them. Police resorted to firing on the mob in which one of the processionists was killed.

Popular support to the freedom movement and the electoral success of the NDF was resented by the French Indian authorities, and Governor Baron tried to weaken the movement by creating divisions among the rank and file of the Front. He lured a few of its leaders like Lambert Saravane, Counouma, André, Edouard Goubert and Mouthu Poulle out of it and encouraged them to form a new political outfit and to please Baron, who was a Socialist, these leaders formed the French India Socialist Party in July 1947.[40] Lambert Saravane, who got elected as the candidate of the NDF, was declared as the representative of the Socialist Party. Baron supported and backed the new party with all the strength of the government machinery—administrative, police and judicial. Goubert considered the Communists as his first and foremost enemies and started oppressing the working class with brute force and muscle power. The French India Socialist Party took a more liberal and pro-French stand of favouring the French Indian settlements to continue under the French Union, while other nationalist elements clamoured for the immediate withdrawal of the French from India.

However, announcement of the Mountbatten Plan of June 3, 1947, which envisaged withdrawal of the British from India before August 1947, electrified the whole Indian environment. The news that the British had decided to leave the shores of India for good, came as a bolt from the blue for the nationalist movement in the French Indian colonies. The locals expected that the

French would follow suit and allow them to join the free united India. On August 3, people of Pondicherry gharoed the government offices and demanded freedom from the French rule. The workers, students and the general public organised strikes and called for *bandhs*. Kamal Prasad Ghosh, the Mayor of Chandernagore, declared on August 4, 1947: "Chandernagore forms an integral part of Bengal and has every right to break its links with imperialist France." On August 9, the French Indians took to direct action to achieve their goal. The public agitation brought the French India administration to a standstill at Chandernagore, where the people sealed the government offices, forced the police to lay down their arms and drove away the French Administrator. The French India Communist Party and the French India Farmers' Federation requested its members to haul down the French flag on August 15 and to hoist the Indian national flag. At Pondicherry, those who attempted to do so were brutally attacked by the police and *goonda* elements. Rangasamy Naicker, President of the Thirunallar Commune, was sacked from his post for hoisting the Indian national flag over the Municipal office building.[41]

However, soon there was a change in the stand of French India Communist Party, as a result of the anti-Communist activities of the Indian Union Government. It started criticising both the governments of France and India as well as their willing instruments in the French Indian scene, French India Socialist Party and French India National Congress, respectively, for not arriving at an early solution to the French Indian issue.[42] It gave a call to the French India National Congress to join the popular movement and promised that it would not do anything to spoil the Indo-French dialogue to find a peaceful solution for the French Indian problem. But, when it found that the Indian Government would not say or do anything that would create problem for its French counterpart and would not hesitate to sacrifice the interests of the French Indian colonies for the benefit of the Indian capitalists, French India Communist Party openly declared that it had lost its faith in the Government of India.[43] The Communists condemned the latter as the government of neo-Fascist exploiters and stooges of Anglo-American imperialists who were bent upon suppressing the human rights of their people and announced that they would try to avoid the merger of the French Indian settlements with the Indian Union, as they doubted the very genuineness of the Indian independence.[44] By taking such a pro-French stand, the Communists believed that they could persuade the French Government to extend the human rights laws of the Constitution of the Fourth Republic to French India.[45]

The leaders of the French India Socialist Party started camouflaging the situation at Pondicherry and tried to gamble with both the French and Indian governments, to achieve their personal ends.[46] In July 1949, delegations were sent to Paris as well as to Delhi to find out the stand of the respective governments. While the French Government assured autonomous status for the establishments within the framework of the French Union after the referendum[47], the Government of India promised that after the merger any changes in the administrative set-up of the settlements would be carried out only in consultation with the public.

On its return to Pondicherry, the *Goubert* group, which dominated the Municipal Councils, resolved to indefinitely postpone the referendum and to accept autonomy offer of the French Government and urged the people to approve it. This was due to behind-the-curtain manoeuvres of the French Indian authorities, who tried to keep the Socialists under their tutelage and the latter's ability to change colour, as and when required. Moreover, the fear that following the Chandernagore example, the people of the other settlements too would vote them out of the Indian soil would have prompted the French Indian authorities and their local supporters to postpone the conduct of referendum in other settlements.

The French and pro-French elements, on the one hand, tried to hoodwink the Indian Government by dishonourable and deceptive political gimmicks, and to suppress the nationalist elements at Pondicherry with an iron hand, on the other. Political violence was patronised and thus it flourished as a profession in the French Indian settlements. The police and army, at the disposal of the French Indian authorities and the anti-social *goonda* elements, at the employ of the ruling party, indulged in subversive and coercive measures. On January 13, 1950, the headquarters of the French India Communist Party at Pondicherry were burnt down, resulting in considerable damage to *Sudandiram,* the party organ, which voiced for the economic liberation of the working classes and the political liberation of the French Indian settlements since 1934.[48] More than hundred shops and houses of the nationalist leaders and those of the merchants' association were set on fire.[49]

To counter the influence of the French India Communist Party on the working classes, the Socialists organised rival labour unions, thereby trying to disunite and weaken the labour movement. Thousands of employees were thrown out of job. This resulted in the mass exodus from Pondicherry and the French Indians in thousands, took asylum in the neighbouring Indian territories. The estrangement of the French India Communist Party and Dravidian leaders from the Indian cause had already weakened the struggle for merger with India. All this resulted in a lull in the mass movement.

Working class leaders of India like V.V. Giri intervened and brought a compromise between the Government of India and the labour leaders of the French India. As a result, by the end of 1953, the French India Communist Party called for united action among all the nationalist elements and accelerated the phase of the movement. An all-party conference was held at Cuddalore to coordinate the freedom struggle. The French India Communist Party launched its direct action on April 6, 1954 and in the following days its volunteers stormed the Thirubhuvani police station and municipal office. Administration of the municipality was taken over by the representatives of the people.[50] A couple of Communist cadres lost their lives when they tried to free Kallaye village in the Mahe region from the French rule. The nationalist leaders organised demonstrations and processions demanding the merger of the settlements with the Indian Union. While the Indian Government hesitated to take action in this regard, the French Indian Government deployed the army brought from Saigon to assist the police and tried to crush the popular upsurge.

Meanwhile, the French India Socialist Party leaders switched over their loyalty to the Indian Union and Nehru had not hesitated to embrace them into the

Congress fold.[51] His government started negotiating with its French counterpart, which was forced to accept the writing on the wall in the end. The agreement for the *de facto* transfer of the French Indian colonies to the Indian Union was signed in New Delhi on October 21 and came into force on November 1, 1954.

In sum, it may be concluded that the working class played a notable and meritorious role in the popular anti-colonial movement for the restoration of political and socio-economic rights of the people of French India. The stand that they had taken differed at different times as its leaders were acting or reacting to various international, national and local developments and compulsions.

## References

1. The landlord and rich peasants numbered 517 in 1857 and 692 in 1858, *Annuaire Del'inde Française, Annie 1860*, pp. 8-9.
2. Called *Panial* at Karaikal.
3. Jaques Weber, *Pondichéry, et les comptoirs de l'Inde après-Dupleix, La démocratie au pays des castes*, Paris, 1996, p. 88.
4. Paul, Bluysen, *Notes de voyage aux Indes: Mes amis les Hindous*, Paris: Jules Taillandier, 1893.
5. Paul, Bluysen, *Notes de voyage aux Indes: Mes amis les Hindous*, Paris: Jules Taillandier, 1893.
6. Jacques Weber, "The Country Trade in Pondicherry in the 19th Century", in *Pondicherry University Journal of Social Sciences and Humanities*, Pondicherry, Vol. 2, No.1 and 2, 1991, pp. 42-43.
7. A Handloom cloth.
8. Pellet Paul. *Atlas des colonies françaises dressées par ordre du ministère des colonies,* Paris: Librairie Armand Colin, 1900, pp. 61-62.

9. Eight to nine *Annas* (40 to 45 centimes) for men, five *Annas* (25 centimes) for women and one *Anna* (five centimes) for children and their wages were assessed on two basic factors (i) work with machine help/related work was assessed at piece rate and (ii) work without machine help was assessed at a fixed rate of wages, (*Sukhabhaviridhini,* 23, November 1922).
10. "The situation of the workers is intolerable. Without mentioning the situation of the adults, whose salaries are often too small for the enormous work required, it should draw the attention of the government that exploitation of the children, knows no bounds. They are made to work in the mills, the temperature of which reaches up to 47 degrees and in which no sanitary measures were taken neither to suck up dust nor to ventilate them, children of ten, nine and even eight years, toil for eleven hours, and they are given two or three sous as daily wages" (*Bulletin du comité de l'Asie française,* August 1905).
11. "It is good to realise (...) that the English managers of Rodier mill did not come to set up thier factory on our territory for the sake of making people earn their living, but precisely for eluding from the English duties and increasing profits this wary" (*Bulletin du comité de l'Asie française,* August 1905).
12. The 19th and 20th century documents, N.A.I., Pondicherry.
13. *La Dépêche Colonial illustrée,* 30, September 1907.
14. *French India Thozilalar Satta Thittangal,* 1937.
15. Geetha, S., "The Role of Tamil Journals in the French India Labour Movement of 1930s," Proceedings of the 26th Annual session of the *S.I.H.C.*, Bangalore, 2006, pp. 644-652.
16. *Sukhabhaviridhini,* 19, December 1914.
17. *Sukhabhaviridhini,* 30, April 1920.
18. *Sri Soudjanarandjani*, 13, May 1920.
19. On 22 and 23 November 1916 a severe cyclone affected Pondicherry and Karaikal which resulted in 307 deaths and caused famine.

20. *Sukhabhaviridhini,* 11, November 1919.
21. *Sukhabhaviridhini,* 15, February, 1 and 15, March 1922.
22. *Sukhabhaviridhini,* 15, March 1922.
23. *Puduvai Murasu,* 14, September 1931.
24. Subbiah, V., Sudandiram *Pon Vizha Malar: 1934-1984,* Pondicherry, 1984, p. 7.
25. *Sudandiram,* 9, December 1939.
26. Subbiah, V., *Saga of Freedom of French India: Testament of My Life*, Madras: New Century Book House, 1990, p. 81.
27. Subbiah, V., *Saga of Freedom of French India: Testament of My Life*, Madras: New Century Book House, 1990, pp. 81-83.
28. Francis Cyril Antony, ed., *Gazetteer of India: Union Territory of Pondicherry*, Vol. II, Pondicherry, 1982, p. 1015.
29. The French India Labour Code provided rights to industrial and agricultural labourers to organise themselves into Trade Unions. Even the Government employees including the policemen secured the right to collective bargaining under this code. The first article provided for the right to collective contract of labour. This was a unique feature which provided for a mutual discussion between the representatives of the trade union and employers and reach a settlement across the table. There were also provisions for conciliation and arbitration. The right to strike work was the most significant provision of the Code.

    Another important provision was the restriction of working hours to nine hours till December 1937 and to eight hours from January 1, 1938. For overtime work, an employee was entitled to one and a half times of his wages and for work during night times between nine p.m. to six a.m. twice the wages. Industries were prohibited from employing women during night times. Moreover, maternity leave with half wages for eight weeks was provided under this Code. Again, 30 minutes per day were granted to mothers to feed their babies during the course of work. Compulsory weekly holidays on Sundays and a fair compensation against accidents too were provided. The most important provision of the Act was that the employers were subjected to severe punishment if they were found to have failed to enforce any of its provisions. (*French India Thozilalar Satta Thittangal*, 1937).

30. *French India Thozilalar Satta Thittangal*, 1937.
31. S. Vijayalakshmi, "Jawaharlal Nehru's Visit to Pondicherry in 1936 and the Labour Movement in French India" in Krishnamurthy, B. ed., India and France – Past, Present and Future, (Puducherry, Centre for Nehru Studies, Pondicherry University, 2006), pp. 41-48.
32. *Sudandiram,* 1943.
33. Subbiah, V., (*Saga*, p.145) maintains that the nationalist leaders of Pondicherry were actually interested in establishing the Pondicherry branch of the Indian National Congress, but in deference to the advice of Nehru they started the *Mahajana* Party.
34. Cyril Antony, ed., *Gazetteer of India: Union Territory of Pondicherry*, Vol.II, Pondicherry, 1982, p. 1245.
35. Subbiah, V., *Puthuvai Manila Desiya Iyakkam,* pp. 16-17.
36. "Combat' (to fight) was organised in Algeria to free France from the control of Germany during the course of World War II. A branch of it was organised in Pondicherry by Julien Adocéam, who came from Algeria. It was in support of 'Free France' movement of Charles de Gaulle and recruited volunteers in French India with a slogan *partent pour de Gaulle* (to join de Gaulle) to free France from Nazi control.
37. *Journal officiel de l'Inde française*, June1946.
38. More, J.B.P., *Freedom Movement in French India: The Mahe Revolt of 1948,* IRISH, Tellicherry, 2001, pp. 96-97.
39. Subbaiah, V., however, accuses Baron, the then Governor of Pondicherry, as the initiator of this political development with the hope of shattering the strength of the freedom movement. He visualises the conspiracy of the Indian

Capitalists in the move of the intellectuals and capitalist elements of French India in opening the branch of Indian National Congress in Pondicherry, at this juncture. Nehru's refusal to such a move of Subbaiah in late 1930s, of which reference has been made earlier (n. 31), need to be juxtaposed against this new development (V. Subbaiah, *Puthuvai Manila Desiya Ikakkam,* 20).

40. It is an irony that the French India Socialist Party was neither ideologically oriented towards Socialism nor affiliated to either French or Indian Socialist Parties. It turned out to be a group of political opportunists and self-seekers and promoters.

41. *The Hindu*, August, 1947.

42. *Sudandiram*, (Pondicherry) 23, January 1948.

43. *Sudandiram*, 9, 15, 30, March 1948; *Sudesamitran*, (Madras) 26, March 1948; *Dinamani,* (Madras) 25, March 1948.

44. *Sudandiram*, 7, 26, April 1948; 15, May 1948.

45. *Sudandiram*, 10, August 1948.

46. N.V. Raj Kumar, *The Problem of French India,* New Delhi, 1951, p. 73.

47. By the terms of the Indo-French Agreement of June 8, 1948, which aimed to settle the future status of the French Indian Settlements to the satisfaction of all concerned, the Indian Government agreed to the French Government's contention that the future status of the French Indian territories should be left to the decision of the people concerned and that their wishes would be ascertained by means of a referendum, the modalities of which were left to be finalised by the Municipal Councils of all the settlements.

48. Subbaiah, V., *Puthuvai Manila Desiya Iyakkam*, p. 21.

49. Raj Kumar, N.V., *The Problem of French India,* New Delhi, 1951, pp. 79-80.

50. Subbaiah, V., *Puthuvai Manila Desiya Iyakkam*, p. 62.

51. *Bombay Chronicle*, (Bombay), 18, October 1954. Muthukumarappa Reddiar, one of the leaders of the French India Socialist Party had the audacity to claim that the recent political history of the French Indian Settlements had largely been the history of the French India Socialist Party and the purpose of his party's historic meeting at Madukkarai on October 17, was "no less than to cease as a party and to re-awaken as the Congress of the new State". He also claimed: "This party took great initiative in the final and only practical phase of the liberation movement".

# Index